D

letts **explore**

Othello

William Shakespeare

Guide written by Stewart Martin

Contents

OTHELLO

IN A VENETIAN STREET, IAGO AND RODERIGO DISCUSS IAGO'S PROBLEMS RELATING TO OTHELLO.

I FOLLOW HIM TO SERVE MY TURN UPON HIM

OUTSIDE BRABANTIO'S HOUSE.

AN OLD BLACK RAM IS TUPPIN YOUR WHITE EW

BRABANTIO ACCOSTS OTHELLO.

KEEP UP YOUR BRIGHT SWORDS, FOR THE DEW WILL RUST THEM

THEY ARE ALL SUMMONED BEFORE THE DUKE AND THE SENATE.

SHE LOVES M FOR THE DANG I HAD PASSO

DESDEMONA ARRIVES AND CONFIRMS OTHELLO'S STORY

HERE'S MY HUSBAND.

THE DUKE EXPLAINS THE TURKISH PLAN

THE TURK WITH A MOST MIGHTY PREPARATION MAKES FOR CYPRUS.

DESDEMONA, IAGO AND CASSIO ARRIVE IN CYPRUS AND AWAIT OTHELLO'S SHIP.

HE TA HER BY PALM

OTHELLO'S SHIP ARRIVES...

MY DEAR OTHELLO...

OTHELLO GIVES CASSIO CHARGE OF THE GUARD.

GOOD MICHAEL, LOOK YOU TO THE GUARD TONIGHT

IAGO GETS CASSIO DRUNK, AND HE ATTACKS MONTANO

ZOUNDS, I BLEED STILL!

NEVER MORE BE OFFICER OF MINE!

CASSIO PLEADS WITH DESDEMONA FOR HELP.

I'LL INTERMINGLE EVERYTHING HE DOES WITH CASSIO'S SUIT...

IAGO SPREADS FALSE RUMOURS OTHELLO.

OH, BEWARE, MY LORD, OF JEALOUSY!

ALONE, OTHELLO BROODS.

IF SHE BE FALSE, O, THEN HEAVEN MOCKS ITSELF.

EMILIA RETRIEVES THE HANDKERCHIEF THAT DESDEMONA HAS MISLAID.

THIS WAS HER FIRST REMEMBRANCE FROM THE MOOR.

EMILIA SHOWS IAGO THE HANDKERCHIEF

I WILL IN CASSIO'S LODGING, LOSE THIS NAPKIN.

OTHELLO'S JEALOUSY GROWS...

BE SURE THOU PROVE MY LOVE A WHORE. GIVE ME THE OCULAR PROOF

IT'S ALL TOO MUCH FOR OTHELLO

WORK ON, MY MEDICINE WORK!

IAGO'S DUPLICITY BEGINS TO WORK.

BY HEAVEN, THAT SHOULD BE, MY HANDKERCHIEF!

DESDEMONA PLEADS CASSIO'S CASE...

DEVIL!

I HAVE NOT DESERVED THIS

IAGO AND RODERIGO PLOT TO KILL CASSIO

HOW DO YOU MEAN "REMOVING" OF HIM?

WHY? BY MAKING HIM INCAPABLE — KNOCKING OUT HIS BRAINS!

RODERIGO ATTACKS CASSIO.

I AM MAIMED FOR EVER! HELP, HO!, MURDER, MURDER

OTHELLO ENTERS...

DESDEMONA AWAKES...

OH, BANISH ME MY LORD, BUT KILL ME NOT!

I'LL NOT SHED HER BLOOD BUT SHE MUST DIE

AND DIES...

IAGO REACTS VIOLENTLY TO EMILIA'S ACCUSATION.

THE WOMAN FALLS. SURE HE HAS KILLED HIS WIFE!

IAGO IS CAUGHT.

I BLEED, SIR, BUT NOT KILLED.

OTHELLO IS OVERWHELMED BY GRIEF.

KILLING MYSELF, TO DIE UPON A KISS

Othello

As the first significant black character in English literature, Othello's Moorish complexion (clearly intended to be black African) would have had an immediate impact on Elizabethan audiences. Shakespeare knew that many of them would be very prejudiced and would have associated a Moor with brutality, ignorance, evil and sexual immorality. The character of Othello both confirmed and contradicted these contemporary expectations in a number of significant ways. Although black – and therefore attracting the audience's traditional Elizabethan suspicion of Moors – Othello is in fact sympathetically drawn. It is the scheming, malevolent Iago who appears as an honest and trustworthy servant, but who is in reality the depiction of evil incarnate. Othello is a highly promoted and respected General at the start of the play, at first a man of calm integrity, a dutiful and loving husband to Desdemona (who is both younger and white) and a pillar of Venetian society. Central to the tragic action of the play is the transformation of this noble character, in front of our eyes, into an irrational murderer under the evil influence of the jealous Iago.

Some critics have commented on Othello's almost passive role in the action of the play – simply a reactor to events – which sometimes makes it difficult to see him in the traditional mould of the Shakespearean tragic hero; someone like Hamlet, for example, who understands and accepts his tragic fate. Other interpretations focus on Othello as a character of extremes: as the noble, heroic, loving innocent trapped and destroyed by the malign Iago, or as the self-admiring, vicious, weak, cruel and arrogant upstart who loves no one as much as himself and who fully deserves his comeuppance.

By the time we first meet Othello (in Act 1, Scene 2) we have had a considerable amount of information about him from others, mostly unflattering. We have been told that 'the Moor', who is also called 'the thick lips', is proud and bombastic and is an 'old black ram' and 'the devil'. Although these views come from Iago and Roderigo, both of whom have cause to resent Othello, they create a strong negative impression in the mind of the audience. On the other hand, the Duke of Venice clearly thinks a great deal of Othello as a General and leader of others, entrusting him with the defence of Cyprus. The previous governor, Montano, is also an early admirer of this 'full soldier'.

As Iago's work on Othello begins to stoke up the furnace of jealousy and his sense of wronged honour, we see a change in his behaviour. Even after the murder of Desdemona, however, we can appreciate the sincerity of character which allows him to accept full responsibility for what he has done and then to deliberately take his own life in self-punishment. However, we might review our initial impressions of Othello as we witness his later actions and be more aware of the possibility that it is his pride which is his ultimate undoing, not his innocence or Iago's malevolence. From this perspective it is easier to see Othello as the traditional Shakespearean tragic hero; an almost perfect character who, through one fatal mistake, finds himself in circumstances which propel him from the height of fortune and regard to complete destruction, and through which he achieves partial redemption.

Desdemona

The character of Desdemona (the name means 'unhappy' or 'evil fate') is the most consistent in the play. She does not change, symbolising the values of helpless good and wronged innocence throughout. Although she is spoken of as a girl and is at first thought even by her own father to have innocently fallen prey to Othello's lust and charms, when we first meet her she seems a mature, confident and perceptive woman who is fully aware of her own feelings and is deeply in love with her husband. Her relationship with other characters is the most important part of her, although she is a credible person in her own right in the play, not a two-dimensional caricature.

She is mature and balanced in her views: she sees a divided duty between her father and her husband at the start of the play; she is sympathetic to the situation of others, like Cassio. She is concerned for Othello when he feels unwell and for his safety when his ship is delayed; she expresses an interest in the opinions of others, like Emilia, but is tactful when they are different from her own views.

Desdemona is portrayed as vulnerable but pure. Her purity has been the subject of some critical dispute, usually revolving around the point (in Act 2, Scene 1) where she exchanges bawdy comments with Iago and where, some say, a coarser side to her character emerges – one more in keeping with Iago's perceptions about all Venetian women. You should consider whether this compromises the view of Desdemona as a pure and innocent woman, or whether it simply shows us that she is not ignorant of the ways of the world and has made a conscious choice not to be corrupt. Her commitment to her husband is not merely spiritual, and embraces the physical and sexual aspects of a loving relationship – something upon which Othello's eventual jealousy and Iago's manipulation of it depend. Iago could not have succeeded at all if we (and Othello) had seen Desdemona as a passionless woman devoid of all sexuality. When she lies about the loss of the handkerchief which her husband gave her, it is clear from the context that she does so out of concern not to upset Othello further, not because she wishes to deceive him or conceal some wrongdoing. Even in her dying words she blames herself for what has happened, not her foolish and jealous husband.

Iago

Like Desdemona, the character of Iago represents certain values and attitudes towards the world which do not develop or change over the course of the play. He is named after the patron saint of Spain, England's great enemy at the time of the play's writing. Iago represents the opposite of everything Desdemona stands for, and the conflict between these two sets of values is a central feature of the play. Desdemona wishes for happiness, peace, reconciliation, order and love, because these are the things which give her life meaning. Iago wishes for death, destruction and anarchy. It is not that Iago does not believe in the things which Desdemona represents, but he feels that life has wrongly denied him these things and so he wishes to destroy them in others. Iago feels that he has been passed over for promotion and that Cassio has been given the position which should have been his. He suspects his own wife, Emilia, of having an adulterous affair with Othello. Furthermore, Iago feels belittled – almost criticised by implication – by the good qualities of others: he cannot endure the 'constant, noble, loving nature' of Othello; and he says that Cassio's 'daily beauty in his life... makes me ugly'.

Iago's feelings are driven by a passion of such intense strength that, even though we might understand his motives, it is difficult to feel that anything other than pure evil could compel him to such extremes of behaviour as a result. Iago also seems to take a powerful, sadistic delight in the damage which he causes. His effectiveness as a character in the play rests upon the ways he is perceived. The other characters see loyalty, honesty and trustworthiness; the audience watches a malevolent – almost satanic – character mercilessly manipulate others with the intention of completely destroying them. Hence Iago's open comment, 'I am not what I am'.

Iago <u>manipulates</u> the perceptions of other characters with great skill, using lies which contain sufficient truth for us to see why it could be that anyone should believe them. <u>He</u> <u>controls</u> <u>the</u> <u>plot</u> for most of the play, and moves Othello towards his <u>cynical</u> <u>view</u> of the world. However, Iago can only achieve his ends through the <u>weakness</u> <u>of</u> <u>others</u>. In this respect *Othello* is similar to the traditional Morality Plays of the period, in which a character must choose between the devil (evil) and an angel (good). Othello has to choose between Desdemona and Iago, and his inability to accept his own potential for love and trust finally destroys him.

Roderigo

Roderigo loves Desdemona and, even though he knows she is married, pays Iago to help him in his attempts to win her affections. Iago <u>dupes</u> <u>this</u> <u>gullible</u> Venetian gentleman to the extent that he becomes persuaded to attempt the murder of Cassio one dark night in Cyprus. (He has followed Desdemona there because he thinks Iago is close to securing her love for him.) Roderigo's <u>foolishness</u> in believing Iago anticipates the way Othello is similarly taken in by Iago's lies and insinuations, and his dramatic role at the start of the play allows the audience to gain an <u>insight</u> <u>into</u> <u>Iago's</u> <u>scheming</u>. The appearance of Roderigo is used at several points in the play to similar effect, as his conversations with Iago are usually accompanied by a soliloquy from the latter, who reveals to the audience even more of his deceptions. The character of Roderigo is not <u>strongly</u> <u>drawn</u>, but we see enough to know that he is a <u>weak</u> <u>and</u> <u>pliant</u> person who, although not without feeling and some moral conscience, is completely within the <u>power</u> of his malign employee. Roderigo would be happy to win Desdemona by any means and, like Othello, becomes <u>entangled</u> <u>in</u> <u>Iago's</u> <u>scheming</u> until it is impossible for him to escape. When Roderigo has some doubts about his venture and suggests backing down, Iago decides, in a coldly calculating way, that <u>he</u> <u>must</u> <u>be</u> <u>killed</u> in case the truth is exposed.

Cassio

As the play opens, Othello has appointed Cassio as his Lieutenant. This is the main source of provocation for Iago's jealousy and hatred of Cassio: Iago feels that, as the more experienced soldier, the post was rightfully his. In addition, he notes that Cassio is a handsome, educated and popular young man, 'almost damned in a fair wife' and with 'a daily beauty in his life'. As a Florentine, Cassio is also something of an outsider in Venetian life – like Othello but less so – and it seems to rankle with Iago that both men have achieved more than he has.

At the start of the play Cassio and Iago meet and we see how Cassio can neither understand nor share Iago's cynical and bitter views, especially about the marriage of Othello and Desdemona. Iago is aware that Cassio's courteous behaviour could be misinterpreted as lust, and uses this to persuade Othello. (Iago calls this 'ocular proof' of Desdemona's infidelity with Cassio.) Next, Iago gets Cassio drunk and consequently sacked for brawling. When Cassio seeks Desdemona's help in pleading his case with Othello, Iago uses this against him as further evidence of an illicit relationship. However, despite these efforts, note that Cassio is the only one of Iago's victims to remain alive at the end of the play.

Apart from Iago and those whose minds he poisons (for example Montano and, later, Othello), all the other characters usually think well of Cassio. But Shakespeare has drawn a more rounded figure for us to see; Cassio's treatment of Bianca can be seen as heartless and his drunken brawling in Act 2, Scene 3, cannot be wholly excused by Iago's scheming. Also note how keen he is to keep Bianca's existence a secret from Othello, because he feels it will not advance his reputation. It is possible to see Cassio's polite and educated manner as somewhat forced – possibly even pompous – on occasions, as in his rather gushing speeches to Desdemona when he seeks her help.

Emilia

As Iago's wife and Desdemona's lady in waiting, Emilia links the two sides of Iago's plot. Eventually she is also instrumental in revealing her husband's malevolence, for which he stabs and kills her. At first Emilia unknowingly helps Iago by obtaining Desdemona's handkerchief, which he then secretes in Cassio's lodgings to use as evidence to Othello of Cassio's infidelity with Desdemona. Emilia seems not to wonder why Iago should want the handkerchief, perhaps because she tends not to concern herself with the more sophisticated thinking which seems to preoccupy and drive other characters.

Emilia is a very down-to-earth woman, whose matter-of-fact attitudes to marital infidelity form a sharp contrast to the very different – possibly unrealistically innocent – standards of her mistress. At the end of the play her directness proves to be Iago's undoing, when she exposes his plotting without thought for the consequences. We can clearly see that while she might be a crude and vulgar character, Emilia is not wicked and has virtuous qualities, such as honesty and loyalty to Desdemona.

Bianca

Although Bianca is not a major character in the play, she has an important part to play in relation to its major themes, especially that of appearance and reality and the way in which men see only the extremes of the whore (or devil) and the pure wife (or saint). Iago speaks of her as a common prostitute: 'A housewife that by selling her desires / Buys herself bread and clothes.' But there is more to Bianca than this, for she has fallen in love with Cassio and is deeply offended at Emilia's accusation in Act 5, Scene 2 that her relationship to him is nothing more than that of a common whore. Although Cassio and Iago exchange amused comments about Bianca's desire to wed Cassio, it seems as though he may have some feelings for her, although he is less than open with Iago about this and conceals her existence from Othello for fear that it might affect his reputation or professional advancement. Bianca's feelings towards Cassio seem genuine and she is jealous of another imagined suitor when he produces the handkerchief which, unknown to him, has been planted in his lodgings by Iago.

Brabantio

As a Venetian senator, Brabantio is upset to learn from Iago that his daughter Desdemona has eloped with Othello. He quickly becomes outraged by the crude sexual way in which the elopement is described, saying that it was foretold to him in a dream. He later expresses his disgust that his 'tender' and 'happy' daughter should have been seduced to Othello's 'sooty bosom'.

Although Brabantio appears only in the first act and is not a major character, the incident with his daughter is significant in that it emphasises contemporary racist feelings towards Moors and underlines Othello's isolation from Venetian society. Brabantio's final words also anticipate Iago's arguments to Othello that Desdemona is deceitful by nature: 'She has deceiv'd her father, and may thee.' Later, we learn that Brabantio has died of grief because of his daughter's marriage.

About the author

William Shakespeare

William Shakespeare was born in Stratford-upon-Avon on 23 April 1564. His father, John Shakespeare, was a glove-maker by trade and a respected member of the community, holding, at various times, several important public offices, including those of councillor, Justice of the Peace and, in 1568, Mayor. Besides his craft as a glove-maker, he was a successful businessman trading in wool and involved in money lending. Shakespeare's mother, Mary Arden, was the daughter of a wealthy local farmer.

It is likely that, as the son of an important townsman, Shakespeare's education began at the town's 'petty' or junior school, before he went on to Stratford Grammar School, where he learned Latin and studied the classical writers, such as the Roman writers Ovid and Plautus. The influence of these writers can be seen in some of Shakespeare's plays, such as *Antony and Cleopatra* and *Julius Caesar*.

In 1582, when he was 18, Shakespeare married Anne Hathaway, the 26-year-old daughter of a local farmer. Their first child, Susanna, was born the following May and the twins, Judith and Hamnet, were born two years later. Sadly, though, Hamnet died in 1596 at the age of 11.

Very little is known about Shakespeare's life between 1585 and 1592, and these are sometimes known as 'The Lost Years'. We do know, however, that by 1592 he had moved to London. He probably left Stratford around 1586–7, and it seems more likely that he joined one of the London-based theatre companies which sometimes visited the town. He would have known that London was the place to be if he wanted to become a successful actor/playwright. By 1592, Shakespeare had established his reputation as an actor and dramatist and was sufficiently well known to attract comment from some other dramatists of the time.

In 1593 all the theatres were closed because of the plague, and when they reopened the following year, Shakespeare had joined others to form a new theatre company under the patronage of the Lord Chamberlain, called The Lord Chamberlain's Men. Shakespeare wrote plays for this company for almost twenty years, and its leading actor, Richard Burbage, played many of the roles created by Shakespeare, such as Hamlet, Othello and King Lear.

In 1599 the Lord Chamberlain's Men built a new theatre, The Globe, on the south bank of the River Thames at Southwark, and Shakespeare was a major shareholder in this venture. In 1603, Elizabeth I died and James I (James IV of Scotland) came to the throne. Shakespeare's company changed its name to The King's Men, and in 1609 the company acquired another theatre, the Blackfriars, in addition to the Globe.

Shakespeare's success had made him a wealthy man, and as early as 1597 he had bought one of the biggest houses in Stratford – he kept close links with his home town even though he lived in London. Shakespeare's father had been granted a coat of arms in 1596, and after his father's death in 1601 Shakespeare inherited this and the rights of a gentleman, an unusual privilege for an actor or dramatist at the time.

During the early 1600s Shakespeare wrote some of his most famous tragedies including *Hamlet, Othello, King Lear and Macbeth*. His last plays, sometimes called the Romances, which include *Cymbeline, The Tempest* and *The Winter's Tale*, were written between about 1608 and 1612. About 1611 Shakespeare seems to have left London and retired to Stratford a wealthy man, though he kept up his connection with London as he was involved in a legal dispute over the Blackfriars theatre in 1615. He died in Stratford on 23 April 1616 and was buried there in the Holy Trinity Church.

In Elizabethan England, theatre-going was very popular and, although the theatres themselves were in London, travelling theatre companies went round the country and were hired by those who wanted a play to be performed as an attraction. Often plays were performed in temporary theatres created in inn yards, as well as at court and in the country houses of the wealthy. The plays, therefore, were seen by a wide range of people from all kinds of social backgrounds.

By the end of the 16th century, theatre-going was well established in England, but the theatres of Shakespeare's time were very different from modern theatres. The majority of them, such as The Globe in Southwark, London, were open-air and, as there was no artificial lighting, the plays had to be performed in daylight, normally in the afternoons. The theatre itself was round or hexagonal in shape, and there was a raised platform that jutted out into the audience. There was a recess at the back of the stage, which was supported by pillars and roofed to form a kind of turret from which a trumpeter signalled the beginning of the play and from which a flag flew, indicating that a performance was in progress.

The stage had no curtain and the main part of the audience stood around it on three sides. This section of the audience was called the 'groundlings'. A few special members of the audience were allowed to sit on the stage itself. In the galleries looking down on the stage and the groundlings, seating was provided for those who paid more to watch the play. These were covered and so afforded protection from the weather.

At the back of the stage, a large tapestry or curtain was hung concealing a recess and openings at either side from which the actors could enter and exit. The hanging might be colourful or dark, depending on the mood of the play. The stage itself was covered by a canopy, which rested on posts or pillars at either side. There was one or more trap doors in the stage itself, through which actors could quickly appear or disappear when necessary, for example in the appearance or disappearance of a ghost.

Behind the stage there were rooms called 'tiring rooms', in which the actors dressed and stored their various items and such props as were used. Although 'costumes' as such were not used, and actors dressed in the fashions of the times, these clothes were often more colourful or ornate and striking than those worn for everyday living. Painted scenery was not used, although props such as tables, chairs, thrones, cauldrons, swords, daggers and so on were used. All the female roles were played by men, as women were not allowed on the stage in Shakespeare's time, so tall boys with high-pitched voices were often trained to take women's parts.

People saw the theatre not only as a place to watch and enjoy a play. but as an opportunity to meet friends, exchange gossip and eat and drink. During performances, beer was often drunk and vendors moved among the groundlings selling various foods and sweetmeats. Elizabethan audiences were appreciative of a good play performed well but, if the play or performance was poor, they would often shout out derogatory remarks, make jokes at the actors' expense and throw things onto the stage – behaviour that is rarely seen in theatres today.

Kenneth Brannagh and Laurence Fishburne in the 1995 film adaptation.

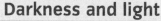

Themes and images

Darkness and light

The role taken by <u>literal</u> <u>darkness</u> <u>and</u> <u>light</u> in the play is connected to the other central image of <u>black</u> / <u>white</u> <u>and</u> <u>angel</u> <u>and</u> <u>devil</u>. As such, the symbolism is not straightforward. Notice, for example, that although three of the five acts occur during darkness or at night – with only Acts 3 and 4 being in bright daylight – it is during the <u>daylight</u> <u>acts</u> that the <u>deceptions</u> <u>take</u> <u>place</u>. During broad daylight, when Othello is certain that he is seeing things most clearly, the conversation between Iago and Cassio convinces him that Desdemona has been false to him, when in fact the two men are speaking about an altogether different woman – Cassio's admirer, Bianca. The play opens amidst <u>confusion</u> <u>and</u> <u>darkness</u>, a confusion which Iago is at pains to increase. At the start Othello's charismatic presence, together with the Duke's judicious carefulness, is enough to resolve the rising domestic and military disorder. By the time we reach Act 5, however, the clear judgement and measured manner of Othello has been destroyed, and the Duke is far away in Venice.

Appearance and reality

The contrast between the way things are and the way they seem to be runs through many of Shakespeare's plays. In *Othello*, as in other great Shakespearean tragedies, this examination expands to encompass issues of <u>conflict</u> between <u>good</u> <u>and</u> <u>evil</u> which draw in almost all the characters. Until Iago poisons his mind, Othello seems to regard appearance and reality as identical. From the start, we find this attitude set against the chameleon-like ability of Iago to <u>blind</u> <u>others</u> <u>to</u> <u>his</u> <u>real</u> <u>nature</u>; he comments to Roderigo 'I am not what I am'. While Othello's 'perfect soul' lives behind a black face, Iago's black heart hides behind a smiling and <u>seemingly</u> honest white face. Only Iago truly seems to know the nature of the man within Othello, although Iago makes a <u>fatal</u> <u>error</u> in thinking that it is possible for him to <u>keep</u> <u>hidden</u> his own designs. As the tragedy unfolds, the darkness within Othello's soul comes increasingly to echo that of his appearance. By contrast, although Iago ironically describes himself as 'honest', he is <u>well</u> <u>aware</u> <u>of</u> <u>his</u> <u>own</u> <u>nature</u> – unlike Othello, Cassio and the others, who <u>think</u> <u>they</u> <u>see</u> a genuinely honest figure in Iago.

Among the major characters, only in Desdemona do we see <u>outward</u> <u>appearance</u> <u>reflecting</u> <u>inner</u> <u>character</u>, appearance and reality as one, although she is continually suspected of being false. It is by persuading Othello of the likelihood of <u>differences</u> <u>between</u> <u>appearance</u> <u>and</u> <u>reality</u> that Iago steers him towards the final tragedy. As Othello's suspicions about his wife grow, his judgement declines. He becomes more willing to condemn and think ill of others – because ironically, he begins to take things exclusively at a particular <u>face</u> <u>value</u>. The construction of stereotypes and the corrosive effect they have on individual human judgement once they become accepted is one of the central issues of the play. Equally, the play concerns itself with many aspects of extreme <u>'opposites'</u>, such as darkness and light, cruelty and kindness, love and hate, greed and generosity, guilt and innocence.

Jealousy

An important concern of the play is with the way <u>jealousy,</u> <u>hatred</u> <u>and</u> <u>love</u> can sometimes be so closely related that an individual's feelings can move from one to the other, whether their relationships are those of husband and wife or lady in waiting and mistress. Desdemona's feelings for Othello are <u>straightforward</u> <u>and</u> <u>unchanging</u>, but those of Othello himself are altered under pressure from Iago.

Feelings associated with <u>jealousy,</u> <u>sexual</u> <u>betrayal,</u> <u>undervalued</u> <u>worth</u> <u>and</u> <u>unrewarded</u> <u>loyalty</u> drive Iago himself, but are also found in other characters and in the relationships between them. For example, when Cassio gives Bianca a handkerchief to work on, she at once becomes jealous and accuses him of having loved another. Emilia is uncompromising in her comments about the <u>attractions</u> of <u>infidelity</u>, of which the jealous Iago already suspects her. Othello becomes insanely jealous of Desdemona. All three relationships have in common the handkerchief and the central role played by the complete <u>lack</u> of <u>actual</u> <u>evidence</u> to support these feelings of betrayal. The relationships between Cassio and Bianca, and between Emilia and Iago, are characterised by the man's evident complete lack of regard for the woman throughout (unlike the relationship of Othello and Desdemona which is, at least at first, characterised by mutual love and respect). Notice that it is the relationship which represents the most elevated form of love which is made to fall, whereas we might feel that the others would have easily survived allegations of infidelity, given that one partner in each is already half convinced of it.

Heaven and Hell

Much of the play addresses itself to notions about the forces of <u>good</u> <u>and</u> <u>evil</u>, the way characters have within themselves aspects of <u>angel</u> <u>and</u> <u>devil</u>, and the relationship of these to Elizabethan notions of <u>heaven</u> <u>and</u> <u>hell</u>. At the start of the play the imagery used by other characters seeks to link Othello's actions with those of the <u>devil</u> – his appearance, his motives, even his use of witchcraft to win Desdemona's love. However, we see in Iago's soliloquy in Act 1 that he seeks to bring about the '<u>divinity of hell</u>'. Several times in the play the nature of evil itself is explored and we are told that <u>evil</u> <u>is</u> <u>most</u> <u>effective</u> <u>when</u> <u>masquerading</u> <u>as</u> <u>good</u>. This is a common idea in Shakespeare's work: evil spreads by the corruption of good, by the poisoning of what is pure. In *Othello* this is achieved by corrupting an individual's perceptions of goodness and evil, so that the <u>angelic</u> <u>aspects</u> of a character are the very things which become <u>twisted</u> <u>against</u> <u>them</u>. In Act 2, Scene 3, Iago says of Desdemona that he will '<u>turn</u> <u>her</u> <u>virtue</u> <u>into</u> <u>pitch</u>', in the same way that he vows to corrupt Othello's view of Cassio's public regard for her – he will 'catch him' in his 'own courtesies'. By the end of the play we find Othello referring to Desdemona as a '<u>fair</u> <u>devil</u>': a word he uses increasingly often in reference to her as we approach the end of the play, although after her death it is Othello who thinks he will be <u>tormented</u> for what he has done: 'This look of thine will hurl my soul from heaven, / And fiends will snatch at it'. He asks devils to whip him and calls upon fate to 'Blow me about in winds, roast me in sulphur, / Wash me in steep-down gulfs of liquid fire!'

At one level the play is a domestic tragedy about a husband and wife who are destroyed by a jealous underling, but the imagery and language show us that their story is also the vehicle for a powerful exploration of the <u>nature of good and evil</u>. *Othello* explores the ambiguity between how things seem and what is real, but does so in a way which allows us to relate this to wider philosophical notions about the <u>nature of good and evil</u> and how reality is constructed, not by what we see, but by the way we think about it. *Othello* is an example of the recurrent interest of Shakespeare and his age in the nature of reality as perceived by humankind.

Black and white

The marriage of black Othello and white Desdemona is at the centre of the play and we are repeatedly reminded of this through the imagery. There are many references to the traditional stereotype of purity and innocence being associated with white, and the devil and evil with black. This stereotype is reinforced at the beginning of the play when Iago shouts out of the darkness to Brabantio that, 'Even now, now, very now, an old black ram / Is tupping your white ewe.' (Act 1, Scene 1) Repeatedly, Iago's comments associate evil and corruption with blackness, and Emilia uses it too when she condemns Othello for the murder of Desdemona: 'O the more angel she, And you the blacker devil.' (Act 5, Scene 2)

The repeated use of this imagery emphasises the conflict between good and evil forces. However, the play also reverses the stereotype: Iago, although outwardly 'white' is inwardly black, while Othello is black in appearance but is inwardly 'fair', as the Duke said. However, as Iago's evil begins to work on Othello, he transforms Othello's inner nobility to evil blackness.

Text commentary

Act 1

Act 1 Scene 1

> *Tush, never tell me, I take it much unkindly*
> *That thou, Iago, who hast had my purse,*
> *As if the strings were thine*

The play opens with Roderigo complaining about the way Iago has behaved; significantly, the argument is about the betrayal of trust, in this case between two friends. This theme runs through the first act. Next we hear Iago telling Roderigo how he will betray Othello because, he says, he has been passed over in promotion and feels let down. We then see Brabantio complaining about how his daughter Desdemona has deceived him by eloping with Othello. Many of the play's themes and images are introduced in this first scene: an interest

in Othello's inner motivations (rather than his outward behaviour or deeds); the presence of secret loves and secret hates; the idea of deceiving others by poisoning their thoughts; references to night, to hell and the devil, to animals and – strongly running throughout the play – Iago's preoccupation with sexual behaviour and sexual imagery.

> *Thou told'st me thou didst hold him in*
> *thy hate.*

Within half a dozen lines we are introduced to Iago's professed hatred of Othello and to the notion that Othello is a poor judge of the abilities and worth of others, as well as being proud and arrogant himself. Othello is much maligned at this point in the

Explore

Remember the impression you form of Othello from this description and compare it with the first impression you form of him when he appears in the next scene.

play, although not mentioned by name. As with the love of Desdemona for Othello, we are given a picture of a situation by others, but must wait for the appearance of those involved before forming our own conclusions.

Iago and Roderigo have come to the house of Brabantio to cause trouble for Othello, whom they refer to as 'the Moor', 'the thick lips', 'an old black ram' and 'the devil'. The traditional imagery of white (good) and black (evil) is reversed in *Othello*, for the noble and cultivated hero who symbolises the forces of life-giving and order is black, while the scheming, murderous and base Iago is the (white) spirit of destruction.

> ❝*I follow him to serve my turn upon him*❞

In this line, Iago claims to 'follow' (serve) Othello only for his own destructive ends. His resentment at Cassio being preferred over him has made him angry, perhaps in part because he has lost face and feels that he has been made to look foolish. Othello may, in Cassio, have made a sound appointment from a technical point of view, but we might wonder why he chose not to appoint Iago. Whatever the reason, the situation has generated destructive forces and we see the same reaction from Brabantio and later Othello himself.

Iago is certainly telling the truth, but not the complete truth, when he gives the appointment of Cassio as his reason for hating Othello. You could make a list of the various reasons he gives at different times, deciding which are genuine. Remember that Iago is likely to lie and deceive in any character's company, though presumably even he tells the truth in soliloquies. Note the use of the word 'ancient': this means 'ensign', the rank below lieutenant and, in Iago's mind, unsuitable for such an old (ancient) soldier as he is.

66 *I am not what I am.* 99

Iago openly admits that he adopts a <u>deceptive exterior</u> and uses other people in order to achieve his own <u>destructive ends</u>. Ironically, Roderigo <u>is not astute enough</u> to realise that Iago is behaving towards him in exactly the same way. Roderigo seems to be <u>such a fool</u> that Iago knows he can safely afford to tell him at least part of the truth. Appropriately, this scene <u>takes place at night</u>, underlining the sense of

<u>concealment and confused perception</u> which runs through the play. Much of the play's action occurs in <u>darkness or gloom</u> – evoking atmospheres of <u>mystery, quietness and danger</u> – and it is not until the start of Act 3 that daylight emerges briefly, before it dims in Act 4 and is <u>extinguished again for Act 5</u>. The gloominess of the present scene opens conspiratorially and ends in loud clamouring.

Explore

Why is it important that this scene takes place at night? What does the night-time setting add to the atmosphere?

66 *Thou art a villain.* 99

This opening comment from Brabantio accurately sums up the situation, even though he is unaware of Iago's villanous core. It is Roderigo who now describes at length, if a little less coarsely than Iago, the circumstances of Othello's elopement with Desdemona. Notice how Roderigo is at pains to convince Brabantio that his daughter is with <u>a 'knave', a 'lascivious Moor'</u>, and is happy to upset Brabantio because it <u>helps his own cause</u>. Brabantio is <u>an important figure</u> in Venetian society and can 'command at most' houses in organising a search. Othello is an important <u>military figure</u> on whom rests a significant part of the state's security and military capability.

Explore

Make a note of the different references to Othello's race as you work through the play.

Text commentary

The strong racist perceptions which others have of Othello, so important later on, are introduced in the most sexually crude and inflammatory way. Roderigo is a willing participant in this scheme, as in all of Iago's other plots, but only so long as Iago is there at the start to strengthen his weak will.

Shakespeare opens the play with a completely negative picture of Othello, skilfully presented to the audience by characters who all have reason to be less than fair and balanced in their views. Iago has lost a promotion because of Othello's choice of Cassio; Roderigo feels deprived of the love of Desdemona because she has eloped with Othello, and Brabantio is encouraged to believe that Othello has stolen his daughter away by force of charms and magic to seduce and violate her and give him beasts of the devil for grandchildren.

Act 1 Scene 2

> **❝He ... spoke such scurvy and provoking terms Against your honour❞**

Iago tells Othello a particular version of the events we witnessed at the opening of the play, suggesting that Brabantio spoke badly of Othello and that it was all Iago could do to prevent himself from killing Brabantio. Ironically, Iago says his 'conscience' will not let him behave this way, even though he has killed many men in war. As always, Iago is at pains to show himself in an 'honest' light, as a noble and loyal servant to everyone he meets.

Notice how Othello will not hide in his house or attempt to suppress the truth: ' 'Tis better as it is'. Othello says his actions and reputation will speak for him, for he is an honourable man, descended from royalty. This claim to royal ancestry would have had a considerable impact upon Shakespeare's audience; this, together with his black skin, makes the character of Othello a striking departure from anything seen before on the stage in this period.

> *My parts, my title, and my perfect soul*
> *Shall manifest me rightly.*

Explore

Do you feel that Othello's self-confidence is arrogance, or does it reflect a calm and rightful sense of his own worth?

Othello refuses to be inflamed by Iago's deliberate attempts to provoke a confrontation between him and Brabantio. He has a substantial opinion of himself which, were it not echoed by many other characters, we might interpret as at least immodest, or at worst as dangerous pride.

We may feel some anxiety that Othello places so much faith in the purity of his own character, when he is neither subtle nor particularly observant in his assessment of others. He comes to doubt his wife's evident loyalty yet trusts Iago implicitly, almost to the end of the play.

Many in Venice seem aware that Othello is visible from two different perspectives: he can be admired as an experienced soldier, a wise ambassador, a strong leader of others and a respected public figure; but as a man he is often regarded with the traditional contemporary hostility reserved for the stereotypical 'black' – he is a Moor and therefore ugly, sexually promiscuous and depraved, cruel and dangerous, and a practitioner of witchcraft who is closely allied with evil and the

devil. Othello's own crisis of confidence, after Iago's poison has begun to work, is rooted in his awareness of these two sides to his public reputation and his private self-image. This scene deliberately confuses the two sides of Othello's nature. Two groups are seeking Othello, each wishing to take him to the Senate.

Text commentary

One seeks him as a great servant of the state, the other as a Moorish seducer: the paradox of Othello is summed up in the confusion between the two. <u>Iago</u> <u>swears</u> <u>by</u> <u>Janus,</u> <u>the</u> <u>two-faced</u> <u>god</u>, that he thinks 'the raised father and his friends' are coming; in fact it is Cassio with news of the General's appointment to Cyprus.

> **❝It is Brabantio. General, be advis'd,**
> **He comes to bad intent.❞**

Again Iago moves into action to try to ensure that a particular version of the situation is seen by others, this time by Othello. Iago frequently describes others and their motives in terms which in fact more accurately apply to himself – here he is the one who has the 'bad intent'. Iago <u>never</u> <u>misses</u> <u>an</u> <u>opportunity</u> <u>to</u> <u>cause</u> <u>confusion</u> and to further his own <u>malicious</u> <u>desire</u> to see confrontation and violence. He even accuses his paymaster, Roderigo, of being behind the scurrilous rumours which Brabantio has believed and here publicly threatens to attack him with his sword although, of course, this pretence is all part of his plan to appear a loyal and trusted servant to Othello.

Explore

Think about how Othello's behaviour here contrasts with Iago's earlier description of him.

> **❝Hold your hands,**
> **Both you of my inclining and the rest❞**

Again Othello orders that there be no fighting, emphasising <u>his</u> <u>noble</u> <u>and</u> <u>civilised</u> <u>character</u> and his <u>calm</u> <u>and</u> <u>dignified</u> <u>manner</u>, and contrasting it with those around him who too quickly give way to unruly passion and violence. It is ironic that Othello fails to take his own advice later in the play and yet here, he claims that 'were it my cue to fight, I should have known it'. As the action progresses, Othello frequently fails to recognise the truth of what is before him and misjudges when he should take action and when he should not.

> **❝There is no composition in these news❞**

The Venetian court's <u>confusion</u> about which of the <u>conflicting</u> <u>reports</u> they should believe is paralleled by that of the audience at this stage in the play, who have heard accounts of the behaviour and character of Desdemona and Othello but have as yet little direct evidence of their own. The behaviour of the Turks, traditionally cast as <u>uncivilised</u> and <u>devious</u> <u>enemies</u>, is <u>parallel</u> to that of Iago.

Explore

The deceptive movements of the Turks links with the theme of the discrepancy between appearance and reality that is explored in the play. Think about other ways in which appearances have been deceptive so far in the play.

Throughout this scene – which effectively turns into the trial of Othello – the Duke is shown as a <u>careful</u> <u>and</u> <u>cautious</u> <u>ruler</u>, who closely examines all the evidence before committing himself to a particular conclusion, but who acts decisively thereafter.

> **❝Rude am I in my speech,**
> **And little blest with the soft**
> **phrase of peace❞**

Othello is a <u>soldier,</u> <u>not</u> <u>a</u> <u>courtier</u>, and is himself acutely conscious of this. He sees himself as <u>straighforward</u> <u>and</u> <u>down</u>

<u>to</u> <u>earth</u> and is therefore at pains to dispel accusations that he used witchcraft or potions to win the love of Desdemona. However, as the action of the play unfolds, we see this man of decisiveness and action <u>increasingly</u> <u>trapped</u> within a <u>tangle</u> <u>of</u> <u>mental</u> <u>confusion</u> which echoes that with which this scene begins, with uncertainty about the actual number of ships and the true destination of the Turkish fleet.

Here, Othello <u>contradicts</u> <u>his</u> <u>own</u> <u>courteous</u> <u>modesty</u> at once by proving himself a <u>measured,</u> <u>charismatic</u> <u>and</u> <u>effective</u> <u>speaker</u>, reinforced later by his description of his courtship of

Text commentary

Desdemona. Notice how, in contrast to Iago, Othello almost always speaks in verse, giving what he says an elevated, sincere and noble ring.

66 *A maiden never bold* 99

Explore

Why might Brabantio wish (or need) to see Desdemona the way he does? Could it be parental nostalgia, or a matter of his being seen in public as a good parent, with a 'respectable' and obedient family?

Brabantio's description of his daughter's character at first sight seems at odds with what we see ourselves when Desdemona enters shortly after. But one of the play's themes is that people are not what they may appear to be; another is that people often see only what they wish to see in others.

We also may understand that Brabantio retains a father's vision of his daughter and continues to see her as child-like long after she has matured beyond childish things.

66 *She lov'd me for the dangers I had pass'd,* *And I lov'd her that she did pity them.* 99

Explore

How much evidence is there in this scene to support Iago's contention that Othello is arrogant and proud?

Notice how Othello seems almost to suggest that Desdemona courted him and that heaven has made him especially for her. We see here a sense in which Brabantio's accusation that 'witchcraft' was used to seduce his daughter might in some ways be right. Othello's past is romantic and adventurous and ranges across exotic foreign lands and peoples of which the Elizabethans were only newly becoming aware.

66 *I think this tale would win my daughter too* 99

The Duke's comment signals two important aspects of Othello's account of his courtship of Desdemona. We see how Othello's 'round unvarnish'd tale', with its accounts of his exotic and adventurous past, is used by Shakespeare to tell the audience

Explore

Notice how easily Iago is able to manipulate Roderigo. With one small exception this is typical of how he controls and uses him throughout the play.

more **about** **the** **main** **character** and increase our sense of identification with him. We are also shown how Othello's **open** **and** **straightforward** **account** could indeed have attracted a well-bred young woman such as Desdemona, thus helping to **counteract** **the** **assertions** of **Brabantio** that her love could only have been won 'against all rules of nature' and by the use of 'some mixtures powerful o'er the blood, / Or with some dram conjur'd to this effect'. There is also another, more subtle point being made, for we see that Othello's courtship of Desdemona emphasises the **power** of **words** upon the feelings of others. Iago plants his **destructive** **seeds** into the minds of others precisely by feigning the kind of honest exterior which Othello has, and by the skilful use of words.

This scene also shows us the **wider** **world** of political and military matters set against the love of Desdemona and Othello. These two aspects of the plot are woven together, and connecting the fate of the lovers with the fate of the nation gives a wider, more universal setting to their bond and raises the final tragedy to a more heroic level.

❝❝I do perceive here a divided duty ❞❞

When we first meet Desdemona we find her – in **contrast** to what we have been told so far – to be **quiet, composed and assured**, not at all the neurotic and lecherous, silly and headstrong young woman others have described. She also shows a **clear grasp of her situation** and is able and willing to answer for her own actions with **clarity and maturity**. Although she has entered into a marriage with an older man of another culture, **she foresees no problems** with this. Later, however, it is her **ignorance** of Othello's **feelings of inadequacy** and weakness which is partly responsible for the tragedy. Desdemona is no different from other characters in this respect – like them, she is unaware of the depths of the **darker side** of human nature.

> *If virtue no delighted beauty lack,*
> *Your son-in-law is far more fair than black.*

Explore

How can you explain the degree of malevolence felt by Iago? Is it in proportion to the wrongs done him by Othello and Cassio?

According to the popular Elizabethan stereotype, 'white' or 'fair' is seen as the ideal of <u>moral</u> <u>correctness</u>. However, Shakespeare <u>questions</u> <u>this</u> throughout the play. Consider in particular the characters of Othello and Iago, and their relationship, to examine where moral 'blackness' lies.

The Duke of Venice <u>symbolises</u> <u>order</u> <u>and</u> <u>measured</u> <u>judgement</u> in the play. Venice was at the time the most powerful commercial centre in the world, with a vast empire based on the wealth generated by shipping and trade. This is why Brabantio is outraged, in Scene 1, that anyone could think of robbery in such a <u>civilised</u> <u>city</u> and why, shortly, the action moves to an outpost of the empire in Cyprus, where the <u>restraining</u> <u>civility</u> <u>and</u> <u>culture</u> of the Venetian court will be replaced by <u>intrigue</u> <u>and</u> <u>baser</u> <u>passions</u>.

> *My life upon her faith: honest Iago*

The play's two central ironies are encapsulated in this one line from Othello, where the certainty of his <u>trust</u> <u>in</u> <u>Desdemona</u> is set against <u>his</u> <u>faith</u> <u>in</u> <u>Iago</u>. His trust in the 'honest' Iago will open Othello's ears to poisonous accusations, while Othello's life will indeed be forfeit as a result of his lack of faith in Desdemona's loyalty.

> *it is thought abroad, that 'twixt my sheets*
> *He's done my office; I know not if't be true*

In Iago's first soliloquy he explains to the audience that although he has no proof of his wife's infidelity, he will <u>behave</u> <u>as</u> <u>though</u>

it **were** <u>true</u>. This irrational state of mind anticipates the way Othello will be made to feel later in the play and gives us an insight into the <u>malevolence</u> of Iago. We also discover that Iago will use the <u>positive</u> <u>character</u> <u>traits</u> in Cassio and Othello to help him to <u>destroy</u> <u>them</u>: Cassio is a <u>'proper'</u> (good looking/complete) man who is known to be attractive to women, while Othello has a <u>'free</u> **and** <u>open</u> <u>nature'</u> and is willing to believe that men are honest if they appear to be so. (Consider the constant references to 'honest Iago'.) Iago is confident that he will be able to lead them both 'by the nose'.

Explore

As you study the play, you should consider the extent to which Iago is correct, but also how far Cassio and Othello are responsible for their own downfall.

> *I ha't, it is engender'd; Hell and night*
> *Must bring this monstrous birth to the*
> *world's light.*

Earlier we saw how Brabantio accused Othello of being in league with the devil in winning the love of Desdemona. In his soliloquy at the end of Act 1, Iago <u>identifies</u> himself with the <u>forces</u> <u>of</u> <u>darkness</u> **and** <u>evil</u> and the audience is shown the <u>irrational</u> <u>hatred,</u> <u>sexual</u> <u>jealousy</u> **and** <u>envy</u> which drive him. We see from this scene that it is not only jealousy of Othello which drives Iago, for he says he will destroy Othello whether his suspicions about him are true or not. Iago is convinced that his is the superior understanding of human nature, all others being fools. He sees himself as more powerful and cunning than other men: this is an important part of his motivation.

Uncover the plot

Delete two of the three alternatives given, to find the correct plot.

1   Roderigo/Brabantio/Lodovico loves Desdemona and has been paying Othello/Montano/Iago to help him court her.

2   Iago confesses that he is jealous of/admires/hates his master, Othello. Desdemona's father, Montano/Brabantio/Cassio, does not know about her elopement and is woken and told about it.

3   Othello is warned by Iago/Cassio/Emilia about Bradbantio's anger. Desdemona's father accuses Othello of using money/witchcraft/drugs to seduce his daughter.

4   The Turkish fleets appear to be sailing towards the Venetian territory of Cyprus/Rhodes/Florence, which it seems they may invade.

5   Desdemona is allowed to travel with/before/after her husband, accompanied by Iago/Cassio/Montano.

Who? What? Why? When? Where? How?

1   Whose description of Desdemona as 'a maiden never bold of spirit' seems in error?

2   Apart from cannibals (anthropophagi), what other strange beings did Othello tell Desdemona about?

3   What different numbers of ships are reported to be in the Turkish fleet?

4   Which character feels that he has foreseen present events in his dreams?

5   Who is encouraged to put money in his purse?

6   Of which character is it said that he 'thinks men honest that but seem to be so', and why is this an important comment?

Who said that?

1   'Thou told'st me, thou didst hold him in thy hate.'

2   'Were it my cue to fight, I should have known it, / Without a prompter.'

3   'I do perceive here a divided duty...'

4   ''tis in ourselves, that we are thus, or thus.'

5   'Even now, very now, an old black ram/Is tupping your white ewe.'

Act 2

Act 2 Scene 1

> ❝ *Methinks the wind does speak aloud at land,*
> *A fuller blast ne'er shook our battlements* ❞

The storm which opens Act 2 serves various dramatic functions. It provides <u>tension,</u> <u>excitement</u> and an opportunity for all to praise the military virtues of Othello. It disperses the Turkish fleet and thus creates a situation where Othello, Cassio and Iago are stationed in Cyprus, but have only <u>domestic</u> <u>and</u> <u>emotional</u> concerns. The possible Turkish invasion can be seen as a <u>dramatic</u> <u>pretext</u> to take the characters away from the ordered world of Venice. The storm also suggests that Cyprus is a much <u>wilder</u> <u>and</u> <u>more</u> <u>dangerous</u> place than Venice.

> ❝ *Sir, would she give you so much of her lips*
> *As of her tongue she has bestow'd on me* ❞

Explore

Is Iago cold and callous towards his wife? Or are his bawdy comments to her here and elsewhere merely the outward signs of a happy, robust and earthy relationship?

Iago's <u>opinion</u> <u>of</u> <u>all</u> <u>women</u> is exposed here, as Cassio greets Emilia with a kiss. When his wife objects that this is untrue, Iago elaborates on what he thinks women are, <u>criticising</u> <u>them</u> for behaving in ways which <u>hide</u> <u>their</u> <u>real</u> <u>natures</u>. Apart from the obvious <u>irony</u> of these comments, coming as they do from the arch deceiver in the play, they may also reveal something of the <u>relationship</u> <u>between</u> <u>Iago</u> <u>and</u> <u>Emilia</u>.

> ❝ *He takes her by the palm; ay, well said* ❞

In this aside, Iago tells us how he will misrepresent Cassio's courteous nature to a <u>gullible</u> <u>Othello</u>. Iago says of Cassio 'I will catch you in your own courtesies', making it clear that <u>Iago</u> <u>knows</u> as well as anyone that <u>there</u> <u>is</u> <u>no</u> <u>real</u> <u>foundation</u> for any suspicion.

Text commentary

Although there is a possibility that he has romantic affection for Desdemona – and possibly for many women, as a young man-about-town – there is no evidence that he behaves improperly towards her as a result.

> **That Cassio loves her, I do well believe it**

This scene ends, like the last, with Iago plotting the undermining of others, this time of Cassio. Notice Iago's apparent bluntness and bluffness in this scene: even when berating his enemies, he still sounds like 'honest Iago'. During this soliloquy, Iago acknowledges the good qualities of Othello and Cassio, and his paranoid suspicion that his wife has slept with both of them. One source of Iago's suspicions seems to be his own feelings of lust towards Desdemona, for he assumes that other men are driven by the same base passions as he is, and thinks that only fools will deny this.

Explore

Choose some good examples of Iago's apparent honesty in his sardonic criticism of women earlier in the scene and in his exclamations to the dupe, Roderigo.

Text commentary

Act 2 Scene 2

> **it is the celebration of his nuptials**

The gentleman reads a proclamation in which it is stated that now that the Turkish fleet has been dispersed all is well, and that a time of celebration is at hand. Significantly, the garrison is given leave to relax, to lower its guard and take its ease. We should recall the connection already made between Iago and the Turks, for the enemy within – in several senses – is busily at work and will disturb the peace in several ways. The proclamation encourages every man to whatever 'sport and revels his mind leads him', reminding us of Iago's previous soliloquy and what he intends to do.

> ❝*She is a most exquisite lady.*❞

Again, we see a sharp <u>contrast</u> between the <u>perceptions of Iago and Cassio</u>. To Cassio, Desdemona is a 'fresh and delicate creature' who although 'inviting' in her manner is also 'right modest', with a voice of 'perfection'. Iago, on the other hand, characteristically sees her in baser terms as 'sport for Jove' and 'full of game', with a look which is pure 'provocation' and a voice which is 'an alarm to love'. The way Iago <u>inflames</u> men by his <u>graphic and base descriptions</u> of sexual intercourse reflects his own preoccupation. Here it echoes the way he spoke to Brabantio at the start of the play.

> ❝*I have very poor . . . brains for drinking*❞

Cassio says he wishes someone would invent some other way for people to entertain themselves apart from drinking, because it affects him badly; he is 'unfortunate in the infirmity' and 'dare not task' his weakness with any more wine, having already drunk some that night. Iago is <u>determined to get Cassio drunk</u> because he is supposed to be on duty that night and Iago has arranged for Roderigo to meet Cassio – seemingly by chance – and to quarrel, so that Cassio will be <u>disgraced</u>. This is a necessary dramatic device: Cassio's attempts to regain favour with Othello with the help of Desdemona will later provide the opportunity for Iago to <u>corrupt Othello's mind</u> with suggestions of his wife's collusion and <u>infidelity with Cassio</u>. Iago here adopts the same tactic he will later use on Othello, that of finding a person's weakness and then exploiting it under the guise of being a loyal friend.

Cassio's drunkenness is <u>comic</u> in its effect and it seems clear that Shakespeare expected the actor to play as comedy the lines where Cassio insists that he is not drunk, together with his

Explore

Think of as many other examples as you can from elsewhere in the play where Iago exploits the weaknesses or natural characteristics of others.

declaration that he 'can stand well enough, and speak well enough'. This and Cassio's 'this is my right hand, and this is my left hand' are clear opportunities for the audience to enjoy his drunken confusion and lack of proper co-ordination. Iago may be seen as a master-plotter, but in truth he is well assisted by the failings of others.

> **"*And let me the cannikin clink, clink*"**

The drinking and singing in this scene form a familiar part of Shakespeare's plays. As well as providing broad humour and amusement for the audience, this interlude forms a dramatic contrast with the following episode of the fight, Othello's fury and Cassio's dismissal from office. We see Cassio persuaded to drink beyond what he knows to be sensible – especially for a man with his own confessed sensitivity to it – in a way which we recognise as a familiar feature of humanity.

> **"*And 'tis a great pity that the noble Moor
> Should hazard such a place as his own second*"**

Montano's comment here about Cassio's alleged habitual drunkenness is ironic, for although he speaks of Cassio, the audience can see that accusations of having an 'ingraft infirmity' apply more closely to Iago. Later, after the fight, when Montano is too hurt to give any explanation, we see how Iago is left to provide Othello with the story of how the brawl began and to put his particular gloss on events.

Othello accuses the brawlers of bringing upon themselves the very destruction of peace and order which the storm prevented the Turks inflicting. He therefore links the brawl with imagery of self-destruction and the behaviour of barbarians.

> **My blood begins my safer guides to rule**

Othello's comment is telling because it <u>anticipates</u> the way he increasingly will come to behave and <u>exposes</u> <u>the</u> <u>weakness</u> which <u>Iago</u> <u>will</u> <u>exploit</u>. Othello is <u>angry</u> at the disturbance and calls upon Iago to explain. We see how the Moor is capable of <u>powerful</u> <u>emotions</u> which his outwardly calm exterior usually conceals and this helps to prepare us for his passion in Act 4.

Explore

Notice how Iago plays the part of one from whom the truth has to be dragged because of his loyalty to Cassio.

Iago gives the impression that things are much worse than he is prepared to admit, that he is putting the best possible face on things so as to minimise the wrong that has been done. Later, he will use this to great effect when describing the relationship between Cassio and Desdemona to Othello in such a way as to suggest adultery.

> **reputation is an idle and most false imposition**

Iago frequently mixes truth, half-truth and outright lies to achieve his ends. Here he speaks the truth about 'reputation' in a way which only he and the audience can fully appreciate. He <u>plants</u> <u>the</u> <u>notion</u> in Cassio's mind that Desdemona would be his best ambassador to ply his suit with Othello, knowing that this will <u>further</u> <u>his</u> <u>own</u> <u>scheming</u>. Notice how the drink has affected Cassio so that he remembers little of the brawl.

> **When devils will their blackest suits put on,**
> **They do suggest at first with heavenly shows**

The identification of Iago with the <u>spirits</u> <u>of</u> <u>hell</u> is reinforced in this soliloquy, where he gloats over his ploy to get Desdemona to speak to Othello on Cassio's behalf. This will allow Iago to 'turn her virtue into pitch' in Othello's eyes. The use of oxymoron ('Divinity of hell') adds impact to Iago's evil. The scene ends with Iago determining to use his own wife as part of his plot.

Uncover the plot

Delete two of the three alternatives given, to find the correct plot.

1 Iago/Othello/Cassio tells Roderigo that Desdemona really loves Brabantio/Cassio/Lodovico but says that she will love him soon.

2 Othello/Roderigo/Iago is persuaded to pick a fight with Cassio while he is on duty and thus disgrace him.

3 A great celebration is held to honour the occasion/consummation/anniversary of Othello's marriage. Iago gets Cassio/Othello/Roderigo drunk and argumentative.

4 Montano/Iago/Cassio argues and fights with Roderigo/Othello/Bianca.

5 Emilia/Iago/Othello tells Montano that Cassio/Brabantio/Roderigo is prone to drunkenness and fighting. As he tries to separate a quarrel, Roderigo/Iago/Montano is wounded.

6 Left alone, Cassio/Roderigo/Iago says he will get Othello to misinterpret this.

Who? What? Why? When? Where? How?

1 Who describes Othello as having 'a constant, loving, noble nature'?

2 Which character has love 'turn'd almost the wrong side outward'?

3 Who has 'poor and unhappy brains for drinking'?

4 Who thinks that Othello should be told about Cassio's 'infirmity'?

5 Who complains to whom that his money is almost spent?

6 Who is 'sport for Jove', according to whom?

Who said that?

1 'As little a web as this will ensnare as great a fly as Cassio.'

2 'Sir, he is rash, and very sudden in choler…'

3 'Well, happiness to their sheets!'

4 'What wouldst thou write of me, if thou shouldst praise me?'

5 'I fear Cassio with my night-cap…'

6 'My blood begins my safer guides to rule…'

Act 3

Act 3 Scene 1

> *You ha' not been a-bed then?*

Iago's entrance and comment to Cassio help to emphasise the <u>continuous flow of time</u> in the drama. The time scheme of the play, encompassing all the action within <u>two days</u>, emphasises the <u>headlong rush of the tragedy</u> and the seemingly irresistible progress of Iago's evil plans. You should notice, however, that occasionally more time seems to have passed. This hidden time scheme allows <u>sufficient delay</u> for relationships to have developed. For example, Desdemona is alleged to have committed adultery with Cassio several times. However, the <u>dramatic reality</u> of the play is that the flow of time both accelerates and slows down as dictated by the playwright.

> *The General and his wife are talking of it,*
> *And she speaks for you stoutly*

Before Cassio has had time to ask Desdemona to intercede with Othello on his behalf, she is already doing so. Thus Iago <u>exploits the natural actions</u> of his victims to their disadvantage. In this scene we meet Emilia for the first time and see that she is a close companion of Desdemona, being allowed to remain while such matters are discussed.

Act 3 Scene 2

> *This fortification, gentlemen, shall we see't?*

This very brief scene has various purposes: to show Othello <u>taking his responsibilities seriously</u>, to mark the <u>passing of</u>

time and to remove Othello from the action temporarily so that he may return to witness Cassio and Desdemona together.

Act 3 Scene 3

> **Ha, I like not that.**

Iago plants a seed which he will nurture throughout this scene. He suggests that the figure he has seen leaving cannot be Cassio, because he is an honourable man who would not stoop to such a <u>sneaking</u> <u>and</u> <u>dishonest</u> <u>kind</u> <u>of</u> <u>behaviour</u>. By suggesting that an action which might seem innocent may in reality conceal something altogether <u>more</u> <u>suspicious</u>, he hints that Cassio has a <u>guilty</u> <u>conscience</u> and then later suggests to Othello what it might be that Cassio could feel guilty about. Iago proceeds with stealth, using <u>insinuation</u> rather than outright lies to achieve his ends. Even Iago's revelation at the end of this scene about Cassio's dream may be the truth, but by then it is too late for Othello to see it as anything but 'proof' of his wife's adulterous affair.

> **As where's that palace, whereinto foul things**
> **Sometimes intrude not?**

Iago speaks of how the purest soul may suffer the intrusion of foul things at times. This echoes exactly what is happening in this scene, where Iago <u>pours</u> <u>his</u> <u>foul</u> <u>poison</u> <u>into</u> <u>the</u> <u>mind</u> <u>of</u> <u>Othello</u>.

> **Though I perchance am vicious in my guess**

Iago again uses the extremely effective device of <u>appearing</u> <u>to</u> <u>be</u> <u>very</u> <u>reluctant</u> <u>to</u> <u>speak</u> <u>ill</u> <u>of</u> <u>others</u> while at the same time managing to suggest that he knows much which would <u>distress</u> <u>Othello</u> <u>if</u> <u>he</u> <u>were</u> <u>to</u> <u>tell</u> <u>him</u> <u>about</u> <u>it</u>. No matter how many dreadful things Iago then says, Othello is left with the abiding belief that he knows <u>more</u> <u>terrible</u> <u>things</u> <u>than</u> <u>he</u> <u>has</u> <u>told</u> and is trying to minimise the hurt to his master, because of his honest friendship and regard.

> **Who steals my purse, steals trash, 'tis something, nothing**

Othello reaches his low point in this scene, for he is threatened in his most vulnerable area – his <u>reputation</u>. Iago is skilful in seeming to know more than he tells and in appearing to speak only under pressure from Othello. Here Iago advances the opposite argument to Othello than he did to Cassio, saying that reputation is everything. Notice how he next advises Othello to beware of <u>being jealous</u>, thereby <u>cleverly planting the idea of being jealous</u> in his mind.

> **I speak not yet of proof...Look to your wife, observe her well with Cassio**

Iago <u>skilfully twists his words</u> so that the fact of Desdemona's adultery appears not to be in doubt – only the proof of it, which will soon be forthcoming. Iago capitalises on Othello's <u>inexperience of Venetian customs</u> when he says 'I know our country disposition well', further encouraging Othello to believe his lies by pointing out how Desdemona has <u>already deceived her father</u> in her choice of husband. This episode also reinforces our sense of Othello's important dramatic status as an <u>'outsider'</u>, someone so unfamiliar with Venetian customs and society that Iago's lies will seem plausible, and who will accept as true the <u>suggestion</u> that <u>all Venetian women routinely commit adultery</u>.

On the other hand, we must be careful not to see Othello simply as an <u>uninformed and gullible fool</u>, for Shakespeare is showing us how all people base their judgements of others on what are really <u>very shaky foundations</u>. This proves to be as true for Iago as for any other character, and we should beware of accepting Iago's view of human dignity as being any more correct than Othello's. For the audience, Iago's determination to see the <u>baser possibilities</u> in the motives of others means that it becomes impossible for us to see any of the characters with innocent eyes. <u>We are made unwilling accomplices in Iago's scheming</u> because we are repeatedly reminded of a particular perspective on human nature. While we might deplore Iago's <u>evil and destructive behaviour</u>, it is difficult not to admire the skill and creativity with which he achieves his ends.

Iago's reference to 'proof' should remind us of how this absolute notion has been used so far in the play. There have been <u>no occasions</u> when proof, in the legal sense, has been forthcoming, and we see how <u>skilfully Iago exploits</u> the characters' tendency to act without absolute proof on many occasions. For example, how certain have we – or characters within the play – been of the sincerity of Iago's support for Roderigo's courtship of Desdemona, the bewitchment of Desdemona by Othello, the destination of the Turkish fleet, the fleet's permanent departure, or Cassio's dereliction of his duty? It is this <u>ambiguity</u> about 'proof', and the way it is so often a matter of how things are seen, which allows Iago to move the criteria for Desdemona's guilt onto such <u>a little thing as the handkerchief</u>.

❝ *This fellow's of exceeding honesty.* ❞

We have had several opportunities by now to see into the mind of Iago through his soliloquies, but this is the <u>first soliloquy given to Othello</u>. This allows the audience to see something which it has not been dramatically necessary for them to see until now: the inner workings of Othello's mind. Until this point the inner workings of Othello's character have <u>mirrored his outward appearance</u>.

Explore

See how many references you can find in this scene to Iago as an honest man and a judge of honesty in others.

Text commentary

45

In this scene – <u>the</u> <u>turning</u> <u>point</u> of the action and the longest in the play – this correspondence between <u>outward</u> <u>appearance</u> and <u>inner</u> <u>reality</u> begins to break down; the only certainty for Othello now is that expressed in the opening line of the soliloquy.

Othello dwells upon what he has come to see as <u>his</u> <u>deficiencies</u> in the eyes of others. The suggestion is that Desdemona may well <u>see</u> <u>him</u> <u>this</u> <u>way</u>: as a <u>black</u> <u>man</u> <u>who</u> <u>is</u> <u>getting</u> <u>old</u> and who has <u>few</u> <u>of</u> <u>the</u> <u>civilised</u> <u>graces</u> of more sophisticated men. Desdemona enters and <u>is</u> <u>concerned</u> that her husband seems unwell – which is true, but not in the way she thinks, for he is sick of spirit, not of body. This episode also gives Emilia the opportunity to <u>pick</u> <u>up</u> <u>Desdemona's</u> <u>dropped</u> <u>handkerchief</u>, which she intends to have copied for her husband, Iago. Note once again that the master-plotter is aided by a huge and unexpected piece of luck.

Explore

What do you think of Emilia's motives? How far can she be seen as an accomplice (willing or unwilling) of Iago?

> *I will in Cassio's lodging lose this napkin, And let him find it.*

In this soliloquy, Iago reveals the key to his success; it is Othello's <u>weakness</u> <u>which</u> <u>will</u> <u>bring</u> <u>about</u> <u>his</u> <u>own</u> <u>destruction</u>. Iago is closely identified with the <u>powers</u> <u>of</u> <u>hell</u> at several points in the play; notice here how he refers to 'the mines of sulphur', echoing the traditional image of hellfire.

> *I think my wife be honest, and think she is not, I think that thou art just, and think thou art not*

Here we see Othello <u>wavering</u> <u>between</u> <u>suspicion</u> <u>and</u> <u>loyalty</u> as he struggles with himself to determine the truth. This proves to be an important <u>turning</u> <u>point</u> <u>for</u> <u>Othello</u>, whose character is

such that he finds it difficult to release a notion once it is formed in his mind. He replaces his existing image of Desdemona only with great difficulty, both here and when he reverses it once more at the end of the play. In desperation <u>he</u> <u>demands</u> <u>certainty</u> – and here we see the fatal weakness in his make-up. The love of Othello and Desdemona has been cast from the start in terms of the <u>absolutes</u> <u>of</u> <u>devotion</u> <u>and</u> <u>purity</u> <u>of</u> <u>passion</u>. Other characters recognise the world they inhabit as one where the base and the noble can exist side by side in themselves and in others. Othello's vision of himself and his wife <u>excludes</u> <u>such</u> <u>compromise</u>, and so when Iago eventually offers Othello 'proof' he is savage in the passion with which he believes her to be guilty.

Othello's status as a tragic hero depends upon <u>how</u> <u>we</u> <u>interpret</u> <u>his</u> <u>behaviour</u> <u>here</u>. Some commentators offer this passage in the play as evidence of Othello's <u>pettiness, instability and suspicious nature</u>, although it may equally be offered as evidence of his feelings of <u>vulnerability, his sense of isolation and inferiority</u>. Equally, we may decide that what we see here is evidence of Iago's <u>mastery of intrigue and deception</u>, which reflects on the essential character of Othello only in a slight way. Othello may be seen as a <u>noble and heroic</u> figure who brings about his <u>own destruction</u> by one fatal error of judgement, or at the other extreme as little more than an <u>arrogant and proud</u> figure who, like Roderigo, is <u>duped by a clever and devious</u> liar. What you decide will depend on the evidence you cite in answering the important question: why does Othello believe Iago?

> **❝** *Give me a living reason, that she's disloyal.* **❞**

Iago realises that he has <u>awakened</u> <u>Othello's</u> <u>wrath</u> and that if he cannot support his suggestions of Desdemona's infidelity he will <u>pay</u> <u>dearly</u> <u>for</u> <u>it</u>. At this point it is interesting to consider whether Iago is thinking rapidly on his feet, or has prepared his answer beforehand as he tells Othello about Cassio talking in his sleep. Othello is by now <u>so desperate to be certain</u> one way or the other that he seems almost keen to pounce upon Iago's account as true. Ironically, the roles of these two characters are <u>briefly changed</u> when it is Othello who is convinced of Desdemona's betrayal and Iago who is arguing in support of Cassio that 'this was but his dream'. Othello's passion has now overtaken Iago's plotting and sweeps the action along.

66 *Do not rise yet.* 99

In a bizarre <u>parody of religious devotion</u>, Iago kneels with Othello as they swear a 'sacred vow' to seek 'black vengeance' against Desdemona and Cassio. We also see how the language of Iago and Othello has been interchanged with their roles. Iago is now clearly <u>the master in the relationship</u>, but speaks of vows to heaven, of service and obedience, while Othello, using language more appropriate to Iago, says of Desdemona: 'Damn her, lewd minx' and calls her a 'fair devil'.

Act 3 Scene 4

66 *Is he not jealous?* 99

The clown begins Scene 4 as a <u>comic interlude</u> between the last scene and this, closely followed by this ironic conversation between Emilia and Desdemona, who is seeking her handkerchief. Disaster is about to strike at the moment when Desdemona feels most secure.

She is certain that Othello has no jealousy within him, as in the place of his birth the sun 'drew all such humours from him'. Othello's comment about Desdemona's 'moist' palm echoes a contemporary belief that this indicated lustful desires, and shows us that he is already predisposed to look for evidence to support his belief that she is unfaithful.

66 *The handkerchief!* 99

We do not know whether Othello's comments about the magical properties of the handkerchief reflect what he really believes, or are just <u>a device to inflate its importance</u> for his purposes here. However, notice how the idea of Othello having used witchcraft to woo Desdemona surfaces again here and serves to remind us once more of his status as an <u>'outsider'</u> and also to suggest that he is now becoming identified with the <u>dark forces of superstition and evil</u>. There is evidence of the changes which Iago has brought about in him.

Explore

Why does Desdemona lie about the whereabouts of the handkerchief?

This is one of the key moments of the play, where the absolute truth from Desdemona might have averted disaster, but it passes ungrasped. Although Othello keeps asking her for the handkerchief, she does not tell him she has lost it. Perhaps she avoids telling him because she does not wish to hurt his feelings; the handkerchief might yet turn up. Perhaps she is frightened by seeing a hitherto unknown and aggressive side of her husband's character. Perhaps she is genuinely hurt at the over-importance he places upon such a little thing. <u>Attempting to deflect</u> the conversation onto the matter of Cassio's reinstatement only makes things <u>much worse</u>. Whichever way it goes, it seems, Iago wins.

66 *'Tis not a year or two shows us a man:* *They are all but stomachs, and we all but food* 99

Emilia at once recognises that Othello's temper is <u>fuelled by jealousy</u>. Her more realistic measuring of human nature reflects

her more <u>matter-of-fact</u> <u>approach</u> <u>to</u> <u>life</u> than that of her mistress. Emilia sees both good and bad in people (mostly bad) but accepts this as the way of the world, whereas Desdemona is <u>astonished</u> at this unusual behaviour from her husband.

> **They are not ever jealous for the cause,**
> **But jealous for they are jealous**

Emilia puts her finger on the danger which Desdemona now faces. She knows, from her broader experience of life, that there is <u>no</u> <u>protection</u> <u>for</u> <u>Desdemona</u> in her assertion that she never gave Othello cause to be jealous. <u>Jealousy</u> <u>is</u> <u>a</u> <u>self-propelled</u> <u>emotion</u> which fuels itself upon its own existence, not necessarily upon the truth. Typically, Desdemona puts Othello's outburst down to <u>worries</u> <u>about</u> <u>matters</u> <u>of</u> <u>state</u>, not the base emotion of jealousy.

> **Throw your vile guesses in the devil's teeth,**
> **From whence you have them; you are jealous now**

Cassio's relationship with Bianca is clearly more than a simple one of customer and prostitute, which is how several other characters see her. On several occasions when they meet, Cassio speaks to her <u>kindly</u>, although it is possible to see him as <u>simply</u> <u>using</u> <u>her</u>. We see in Act 4, Scene 1 that when Cassio speaks to Iago about Bianca he laughs at the suggestion that their relationship is serious and calls her a <u>'bauble'</u> who has convinced herself that he will marry her. You may feel that Shakespeare left the relationship between Cassio and Bianca deliberately ambiguous, offering the audience the possibility that Cassio is an experienced and worldly man. Notice how the handkerchief has <u>provoked</u> <u>another</u> <u>heated</u> <u>exchange</u> – this time from a woman's perspective – about unwarranted jealousy.

Uncover the plot

Delete two of the three alternatives given, to find the correct plot.

1   *Cassio/Iago/Othello has arranged for some musicians to serenade Othello and Desdemona the morning after their nuptial celebrations.*

2   *Desdemona has already begun to love/plead for/miss Cassio. She pleads with Brabantio/Othello/the Duke on Cassio's behalf.*

3   *Iago skilfully steers Othello's feelings towards jealousy/anger/murder about Cassio's relationship with Desdemona.*

4   *Emilia gives the handkerchief to Iago/Roderigo/Montano.*

5   *Iago tells Othello that Cassio has talked to him/to Bianca/in his sleep about his love for Desdemona and that Iago has seen him wiping his face/eyes/beard with her handkerchief.*

Who? What? Why? When? Where? How?

1   *What is spotted with strawberries?*

2   *Who often accompanied Othello when he went to woo Desdemona?*

3   *How does the handkerchief get into Cassio's lodgings?*

4   *Who was going to whose house when she met him on her way there?*

5   *From whom does Othello say his mother originally got the handkerchief?*

6   *According to Iago, why was he awake to hear Cassio talk in his sleep about Desdemona?*

Who said that?

1   *'Who steals my purse, steals trash…'*

2   *'My wayward husband hath a hundred times / Woo'd me to steal it.'*

3   *'They are not ever jealous for the cause, / But jealous for they are jealous.'*

4   *'you are jealous now / That this is from some mistress.'*

5   *'I speak not yet of proof.'*

6   *'and when I love thee not, / Chaos is come again.'*

Act 4

Act 4 Scene 1

> **To be naked with her friend abed,**
> **An hour, or more, not meaning any harm?**

Again we join a scene <u>part-way</u> <u>through</u> <u>a</u> <u>conversation</u>, a device which Shakespeare uses several times in this play to engage our attention and increase the tension. Iago is now much <u>bolder</u> than before, because he has passed the dangerous moment when Othello swayed between trust in his wife's fidelity and suspicion of her honour. Iago now poisons Othello's mind with pictures of his wife in bed with Cassio, then attempts to persuade him that this may be but innocent pleasure. Understandably enough, Othello finds this suggestion preposterous, but we should note how skilfully Iago allows Othello's imagination to do his dirty work for him.

> **Lie with her, lie on her?**

Othello falls prey to Iago's <u>evil</u> <u>influence</u>. He rejects the possibility of <u>trusting</u> <u>his</u> <u>own</u> <u>feelings</u> of love for Desdemona

and is instead seduced by Iago's jealousy and evil. Notice how Iago is subtly identified with <u>satanic</u> <u>evil</u> at several points in the play, as here when Othello cries 'O devil!' and falls down. Iago, indifferent to Othello's condition, immediately replies 'Work on, / My medicine, work.' The calm and rational Othello of the earlier scenes is now completely gone and we see contrasted Othello's mental torture and Iago's unfeeling reaction to it.

> **Stand you awhile apart,**
> **Confine yourself but in a patient list**

Iago tells Othello to conceal himself so that he may overhear for himself the tale of how Cassio committed adultery with Desdemona. Othello's <u>willingness</u> to indulge in spying is another mark of the <u>depths</u> to which he has already sunk. Iago says that Cassio regards his sexual intercourse with Desdemona as a matter for 'jeers', 'gibes, and notable scorns', suggesting that he has treated her – and that she has behaved – as <u>less than a common prostitute</u>.

In fact, the conversation between Iago and Cassio revolves around Cassio's mistress Bianca. Not for the first time, Iago will use Cassio's <u>public behaviour</u> against him. Notice how Othello's thinking is now constructed almost entirely out of the material <u>provided for him by Iago</u> and how he misreads every single element of Cassio's behaviour.

❝How shall I murder him, Iago? ❞

Othello's only thought now is of how he should <u>kill Cassio</u>; he has <u>no doubt</u> left in his mind as to the other's guilt. Othello also considers Desdemona's qualities, his speech and emotions swooping wildly between the <u>extremes</u> of a 'fine woman' who is 'delicate with her needle', and 'an admirable musician' and a woman who should 'rot, and perish, and be damned to-night'. In a gruesome echo of the kind of language we have come to associate most with Iago, Othello says he will <u>'chop her into messes'</u>. Iago advises him instead to 'strangle her in her bed'.

❝I have not deserv'd this. ❞

The arrival of Lodovico with a message from Venice distracts Othello for a moment but, on hearing Desdemona express pleasure that <u>Cassio may be made Governor</u> because Othello is summoned back to Venice, he <u>strikes her</u>. Othello then proceeds to <u>humiliate</u> Desdemona in front of Lodovico as he sarcastically demonstrates how 'obedient' she is. This is the most <u>unsympathetic</u> <u>side</u> <u>of</u> <u>Othello</u> and reminds us again of the stereotype of the 'cruel Moor' which Iago attempted to pin on him at the start of the play. The rest of Othello's speech is a <u>confused</u> <u>mixture</u> of insults directed at Desdemona and matters contained in the letter from Venice.

Explore

Look at the way Othello's use of language here reflects his confused state of mind.

Lodovico's comments about Othello's strange behaviour give Iago the <u>perfect</u> <u>opportunity</u> to undermine his stature further by suggesting – in a reversal of his own self-description earlier in the play – that 'He's that he is'. Iago carefully avoids offering any description of what he thinks is wrong with Othello, being content to allow others to draw the 'obvious' conclusion for themselves.

Act 4 Scene 2

❝ You have seen nothing, then? ❞

Othello questions Emilia in an attempt to verify his suspicions, but no matter how devoutly she swears that her mistress is honest his mind is made up. Othello <u>assumes</u> that if Emilia is telling the truth this must prove how <u>devious</u> <u>and</u> <u>secretive</u> Desdemona has been. His greeting to his wife: 'Pray, chuck, come hither' has an <u>ominous</u> <u>and</u> <u>cold</u> <u>ring</u> <u>to</u> <u>it</u>, following his harsh treatment of her in the last scene.

**❝ Had it pleas'd heaven
To try me with affliction ❞**

Throughout this speech, as Othello explains his feelings to Desdemona, notice how he <u>concentrates</u> <u>on</u> <u>himself</u>: his honour, his position and his happiness. Some commentators see this as

clear evidence that Iago was right to accuse Othello of <u>arrogant</u> <u>selfishness</u> and that he is in reality <u>concerned</u> <u>only</u> <u>with</u> <u>himself</u>. Others suggest that this speech is good evidence of Othello's <u>feelings of</u> <u>insecurity</u>, his perception that as a Moor he is an outsider who is never really <u>accepted</u> <u>into</u> <u>Venetian</u> <u>society</u> and is therefore always acutely conscious of his <u>own</u> <u>failings and isolation</u> in the eyes of others. The imagery Othello uses about Desdemona <u>contrasts</u> <u>vividly</u> with that at the start of the play: his life, his soul has now become the dark pit or 'cistern' where 'foul toads' breed.

> *How have I been behav'd, that he might stick*
> *The smallest opinion, on my greatest abuse?*

Desdemona cannot understand why Othello is determined to turn everything she says against her. Othello has <u>twisted</u> <u>the</u> <u>words</u> she uses in just the way Iago does, emphasising the way his thinking now works along the same lines of that of his <u>unrecognised</u> <u>enemy</u>. Typically, when she summons Iago to explain Othello's strange behaviour, he offers nothing.

> *I will be hang'd, if some eternal villain…*
> *Have not devis'd this slander*

True to form, the perceptive Emilia hits upon <u>the</u> <u>truth</u> with a suddenness which seems to startle Iago, who declares that 'there is no such man, it is impossible'.

In an echo of the earlier scene where Iago and Othello knelt to swear their common purpose in vengeance and hate, Desdemona here kneels to <u>vow</u> <u>her</u> <u>love</u> <u>and</u> <u>loyalty</u> to her husband. Both husband and wife have now knelt before Iago and put their future wellbeing into his stewardship. Desdemona's open and innocent feelings for Othello also <u>contrast</u> <u>sharply</u> with her husband's, emphasising that it is he who has suffered the greater fall in stature. Ironically, both Desdemona and Emilia here <u>call</u> <u>for</u> <u>help</u> to the one person who is <u>most</u> <u>to</u> <u>blame</u> for creating the situation.

> **❝ *I do not find that thou deal'st justly with me.* ❞**

Although Roderigo finally seems to have realised that Iago <u>has</u> <u>duped</u> <u>him</u>, he is <u>easily</u> <u>persuaded</u> that Iago is very close to obtaining the 'enjoyment' of Desdemona for him. Such is Roderigo's <u>willingness</u> <u>to</u> <u>believe</u> what Iago tells him that he will grasp at any chance that it may be true, however unsupported. In this respect, Roderigo's behaviour anticipates that of Othello, of whom he is a lesser echo. Iago is usually successful not only because of the <u>skill</u> <u>of</u> <u>his</u> <u>plots</u>, but because of the <u>weakness</u> <u>of</u> <u>his</u> <u>victims</u>. Iago therefore easily persuades Roderigo that he must kill Cassio.

Act 4 Scene 3

> **❝ *Get you to bed on the instant* ❞**

It would be customary for a young woman of social position to have her maid sleep close to her mistress, usually in a nearby room or passage, but Othello orders her to be <u>dismissed</u>. Before they part for the night we see them discuss the events of the day in this short, sad scene.

Desdemona's <u>love</u> for her husband is emphasised again, as is her <u>innocent</u> <u>lack</u> <u>of</u> <u>understanding</u> of the depth of Othello's feelings. However, we should note the ominous reference she makes to wanting Emilia to use her bed linen as <u>her</u> <u>death</u> <u>shroud</u>. This <u>foreshadows</u> the way Desdemona's bed will indeed shortly become her grave. Her song is a lament for a woman who finds sadness in love, and Desdemona's itching eyes 'bode weeping' for such a woman in ways she cannot know, but which the audience can anticipate.

> 66 *But I do think it is their husbands' faults*
> *If wives do fall* 99

In this conversation between Emilia and Desdemona we see highlighted the <u>differences</u> <u>in</u> <u>character</u> between the two. Desdemona sees that love could never be compromised, whereas Emilia feels that she could <u>succumb</u> <u>to</u> <u>lust</u> if the reward were large enough. Emilia is at pains to point out that she would not be unfaithful for mere trinkets or small favours, nor would she wish her behaviour to become known, but that she considers herself reasonably moral.

Text commentary

Quick quiz 4

Uncover the plot

Delete two of the three alternatives given, to find the correct plot.

1   Iago tells Othello that Cassio has denied/admitted/bragged about committing adultery with Desdemona. Othello faints/laughs/is silent.

2   Othello agrees to arrange/spy on/attend a meeting between Iago and Cassio when they will talk about Desdemona. At the meeting Iago talks to Cassio about Bianca/Emilia/Cecilia.

3   Lodovico/Montano/Brabantio arrives from Venice/Rhodes/Cyprus to say that Othello must return and that Cassio/Iago/Roderigo is to govern in his absence.

4   Desdemona is pleased and Othello strikes/kisses/embraces her. Iago says that Othello's behaviour these days is often loving/unkind/distracted.

5   Othello closely questions Emilia/Bianca/Montano about Desdemona's behaviour. Othello accepts/is suspicious of/ignores his wife's explanations.

Who? What? Why? When? Where? How?

1   Who in this act feels that he has not been justly dealt with by Iago?

2   Desdemona wonders whether itching eyes foretell what condition?

3   When Othello commands Desdemona to go to bed, what else does he also tell her to do?

4   Iago tells Roderigo that Othello has been commanded to go to what country?

5   In whose company does Othello strike his wife?

Who said that?

1   'Stand you awhile apart, / Confine yourself but in a patient list.'

2   'How shall I murder him…?'

3   'This is a subtle whore, / A closet, lock and key, of villainous secrets.'

4   'Fie, there is no such man, it is impossible.'

5   'Was this fair paper, this most goodly book, / Made to write "whore" on?'

Act 5

Act 5 Scene 1

> ❝'Tis but a man gone: forth, my sword, he dies.❞

Explore

Why do you think it is important that this scene takes place in darkness? How does the language of the text emphasise just how complete the darkness is?

This scene echoes that at the start of the play, where Iago and Roderigo met at night to plot their earlier intrigue and treachery.

With dramatic irony Cassio calls out to Iago, of all characters, to help save him from the villains who have sought to undo him. Iago had hoped that Cassio and Roderigo would kill each other so that he might be rid of both of them, but takes advantage of the darkness to murder the wounded Roderigo in cold blood. Notice how even at this stage the references to 'honest' Iago abound, and the irony with which Iago calls Cassio's attackers 'treacherous villains'.

Shakespeare uses the rapid action of this scene, with characters continually coming and going, and with short and broken lines of speech, to emphasise the confusion within the minds of characters. Significantly, it is Othello's mistake in thinking that Iago has killed Cassio that spurs him on to murder Desdemona. Like his other mistaken perceptions, this one will also lead Othello into further self-destruction.

> ❝This is the night
> That either makes me, or fordoes me quite.❞

Iago's aside here emphasises for the audience the critical importance of the next part of the play, upon which everything hangs, and this increases the tension as we move into the final scene.

Act 5 Scene 2

> ❝ *Put out the light, and then put out the light* ❞

In a significant dramatic echo, we see Othello enter from the <u>darkness</u> <u>with</u> <u>a</u> <u>light</u>, just as did Iago in the last scene. The <u>connection</u> between these two characters is that the will of one has come to rule the heart of the other. There is also a <u>dramatic</u> <u>irony</u> in the fact that Othello, whose actions have been overwhelmed by the evil of Iago, is bringing illumination into the darkness. Like Iago, Othello has come to <u>destroy</u> <u>goodness</u>,

although he actually sees himself as Desdemona's redeemer. Othello says of the light that he carries that he 'can again thy former light restore' if he should choose, but that if he kills the sleeping Desdemona he cannot make her 'light relume'. He understands the <u>enormity</u> <u>of</u> <u>the</u> <u>action</u> which he is contemplating, but cannot rid himself of the <u>emotional</u> <u>turmoil</u> which he knows is driving him to act. This complex play on the imagery of light and dark as <u>symbols</u> of goodness and evil therefore echoes the way the darkness of Othello's soul and the blackness of his skin are used to represent his <u>inner</u> <u>confusion</u> and, earlier in the play, were used to emphasise his outer grace. The whiteness of Desdemona's skin here symbolises her <u>inner</u> <u>purity</u> and <u>innocence</u>, which Othello, ironically, says he cannot bear to mark. Notice also the use of other <u>opposites</u> <u>in</u> <u>the</u> <u>language</u>, as when Othello says that Desdemona's sweetness has been 'fatal', that he weeps 'cruel tears' because his murderous act is 'heavenly' ('it strikes where it does love'), and that he is both cruel and merciful in what he is doing.

Explore

What is the significance of Othello's reference to 'putting out the light'? Think about how this image links to other images in the play.

Othello sees his killing of Desdemona as <u>'justice'</u> for her foul deeds. He is angry when she denies any wrongdoing because 'thou…makest me call what I intend to do/A murder, which I thought a sacrifice'. There is a strong mixture in the scene of the <u>public figure</u> of Othello, doing his <u>duty</u>, and the <u>intensely personal emotions</u> of the man: Desdemona's skin is 'smooth, as monumental alabaster', she is 'rose', and her 'balmy breath' almost persuades him to abandon his act. Although Othello characterises his deed as 'justice' it is significant that, unlike the Duke of Venice, he will hear only <u>one side</u> of the story. He <u>rejects</u> Desdemona's pleas to call Cassio and ask him whether she speaks the truth in the mistaken belief that he has been killed.

> **"Good gentlemen, let me have leave to speak, 'Tis proper I obey him, but not now 99**

Emilia insists on being allowed to speak, in spite of her husband's <u>attempts to quieten</u> her. By her actions here Emilia reveals that she is an <u>honest</u> character not without moral standards. She realises that Iago has until now relied upon her unthinking obedience as a shield and out of a sense of <u>shock and horror</u>, she vigorously <u>exposes his lies</u>. Notice how, after Iago has stabbed her and she lies dying, the <u>parallels</u> between Emilia and Desdemona are echoed when she sings part of the willow song which her mistress sang in Act 4, Scene 3.

Explore

Think about your responses to the character of Emilia. Is she a foolish woman who only realises the true nature of her husband when it is too late, or is she another victim skilfully manipulated by Iago?

Both women have been <u>forsaken and killed</u> by their husbands. Emilia's faith in Desdemona is unquestioning to the last, her reaction to the news of Othello's suspicion being that <u>he is foolish</u> to think so. Emilia seems to have had the kind of <u>implicit trust</u> in Desdemona's purity which we might have expected from Othello, hinting that – unlike Othello – her robust and worldly-wise attitude may have made her immune to the kind of character assassination which Iago practised on Othello.

> **I look down towards his feet, but that's a fable –
> If that thou be'st a devil, I cannot kill thee.**

Othello emphasises the idea, which runs through the play, that Iago is the personification of the **devil himself**. Although Othello wounds Iago with his sword, it is dramatically significant that he does not in fact kill him, as Iago gloatingly points out: 'I bleed, sir, but not killed' are almost the last words he speaks. While Othello may have been an **outsider** because of his military background, his culture and the colour of his skin, we see at the end of the play that **Iago is now isolated**; he is morally and spiritually excluded from society. Iago's evil is emphasised at the end of the play, but what is important is not just that an evil troublemaker has been caught, for what Iago has destroyed in Othello and Desdemona is the potential for harmony and goodness in the world.

> **I kiss'd thee ere I kill'd thee – no way but this,
> Killing myself, to die upon a kiss.**

Why does Othello take his own life? You may feel that his suicide is the only **courageous, soldierly option** open to him, or you may think that in his despair he escapes into death because his **spirit is broken**. It is perhaps a contradictory mixture of both which we witness here, reinforcing again the play's central theme of the ambiguity which exists between **appearance and reality** and underlining the impossibility of ever knowing for certain the real **motives of others**, and perhaps of ourselves.

Explore

Think about Othello's claim that he is 'one, not easily jealous'. How do you respond to this? What do you think he means by it?

In his death Othello seems to **regain** some of his **earlier nobility** in a way which echoes Macbeth – both men regain a clearer and saner perspective on the world only when it is too late. Othello dies declaring his love for Desdemona with a kiss.

Uncover the plot

Delete two of the three alternatives given, to find the correct plot.

1   On his way back from the house of Desdemona/Emilia/Bianca at night, Cassio/Montano/Othello is attacked by Lodovico/Roderigo/Brabantio, whom he wounds.

2   Cassio/Montano/Othello is then wounded by Roderigo/Othello/Iago.

3   Othello says he will kill the sleeping Desdemona but not cause her pain/destroy her beauty/waken her.

4   He says the handkerchief/her confession/Cassio's death is proof of her guilt and strangles/smothers/stabs her.

5   Othello eventually realises what has happened and attacks Iago. Iago blames/stabs/hits Emilia, who dies/faints/escapes.

6   The wounded Cassio/Roderigo/Lodovico enters with the captured Iago. Iago refuses to speak/confess/return to Venice.

Who? What? Why? When? Where? How?

1   What is Desdemona's final request to Othello?

2   Which two characters are plotting together as this act opens?

3   What are Desdemona's last words?

4   Of what did Brabantio die?

5   Who is crying out to be let in as Othello kills Desdemona?

6   Who kills Roderigo?

Who said that?

1   'I do suspect this trash / To bear a part in this...'

2   'Tis proper I obey him, but not now.'

3   'Fie, / your sword upon a woman?'

4   'Thou hast not half the power to do me harm / As I have to be hurt.'

5   'What should such a fool / Do with so good a woman?'

6   'Tis but a man gone: forth, my sword, he dies.'

- To prepare for an exam, you should read the text through at *least twice*, preferably *three times*. In order to answer an exam question you need to know the text very well.

- When preparing a play, such as *Othello*, you should try to see a performance of it. If you cannot see a live performance on stage, you should watch it on video. There are several versions available and you should be able to get a copy through your local library.

- If you are studying the text for an 'open book' exam, make sure that you take your copy with you. However, do not rely on it too much – you haven't got time. If you are not allowed to take the text in with you, you will need to memorise brief quotations.

- Read all the questions carefully before deciding which one you are going to answer. Choose the question that best allows you to demonstrate your understanding and personal ideas.

- Make sure that you understand exactly what the question is asking you to do.

- Plan your answer carefully before starting to write your essay (see page 70).

- Always begin your answer with a short introduction which gives an overview of the topic. Use your plan to help keep you focused on the question as you write the essay. Try to leave enough time to write a brief conclusion.

- Remember to use the **point–quotation–comment** approach, where you make a point, support it with a short quotation, then comment on it. Use short and relevant quotations – do not waste time copying out chunks of the text.

- Make sure that you know how much time you have for each question and stick to it.

- Leave enough time at the end of the exam to check your work through carefully and correct any spelling or other mistakes that you have made.

- Timing is not as crucial for coursework essays, so this is your chance to show what you can really do, without having to write under pressure. Do not leave your coursework essays until the last minute though. If you have to rush your work it is unlikely to be the best you can produce.

- Coursework allows you to go into more detail and develop your ideas in greater depth. The required length of assignments varies, and your teacher will advise you on this.

- If you have a choice of title, make sure you choose one which you are interested in and which gives you the chance to develop your ideas.

- Plan your essay carefully (see page 70). Refer to your plan and the essay title as you write, to check that you are staying on course.

- Use quotations in your essay, but beware of using them **too frequently** or making them **too long**. Often, the best quotes are just one or two words or short phrases. Make sure that they are relevant to the points that you are making.

- If your topic requires it, use appropriate background information and put the text in a cultural and historical context. Remember, though, that the text itself should be at the centre of your essay.

- Include a short conclusion which sums up the key points of your ideas.

- Do not copy any of your essay from another source, e.g. other notes or the Internet. This is called plagiarism, and it is very serious if the exam board find that you have done this.

- If you have used sources, list them in a bibliography at the end of the essay.

- If you are allowed to word process your essay, it will be easier to make changes and to re-draft it.

Writing essays

> *But I will wear my heart upon my sleeve*
> *For daws to peck at: I am not what I am.*
> (Act 1, scene 1)

These lines are spoken by Iago early in the play, when he is explaining to Roderigo how he is only appearing to serve Othello but really he is serving his own ends. The quotation can be used to show how Iago is not what he appears to be and to illustrate the difference between appearance and reality.

> *Even now, now, very now, an old black ram*
> *Is tupping your white ewe.* (Act 1, scene 1)

These lines are spoken by Iago when he shouts from the darkness to tell Brabantio that Othello has seduced his daughter. The quotation can be used to illustrate Iago's use of crude, sexual language, the racist overtones of the language and the ways that he is able to use language in order to manipulate the responses of other characters.

> *Now by heaven,*
> *My blood begins my safer guides to rule.* (Act 2, scene 3)

These lines are spoken by Othello when he has stopped the brawl involving the drunken Cassio. He is becoming angry because he cannot get a straight answer as to how the brawl started. The quotation can be used to show how Othello can become angry and, when he does, how his emotions can overcome his reason. This episode foreshadows exactly what happens when he becomes jealous.

> *Excellent wretch! Perdition catch my soul*
> *But I do love thee; and when I love thee not,*
> *Chaos is come again.*   *(Act 3, scene 3)*

These lines are spoken by Othello just before Iago begins to poison his mind against Desdemona. The quotation can be uses to show the intensity of Othello's feelings towards Desdemona. They also illustrate dramatic irony because this is exactly what happens – when Othello ceases to love Desdemona his world falls apart.

> *I had rather be a toad,*
> *And live upon the vapour of a dungeon,*
> *Than keep a corner in the thing I love*
> *For others' uses.*   *(Act 3, scene 3)*

These lines are spoken by Othello when his mind is beginning to be corrupted by Iago's insinuations. The quotation can be used to illustrate how Othello's language and imagery is becoming debased from the noble poetry of the earlier scenes.

> *O perjured woman, thou dost stone my heart*
> *And mak'st me call what I intend to do*
> *A murder, which I thought a sacrifice.*
> *(Act 5, scene 2)*

These lines are spoken by Othello just before he murders Desdemona. The quotation can be used to show how Othello feels that killing Desdemona is a sacrifice that he must make in the name of justice.

1. *Iago has been described as 'a motiveless malignity'. What do you think about him as a character in the play and why do you think he acts as he does?*

2. *How far does the success of Iago's plot depend on luck and how far is it a result of skilful planning?*

3. *How does Shakespeare use two distinct time schemes in the play? Why do you think he does this?*

4. *Some critics have said that there are only three characters of interest in the play, Othello, Iago and Desdemona. Which other characters have interested you and why? You should write about **two** or **three** characters in your answer.*

5. *Examine the importance of Shakespeare's use of soliloquies in Othello.*

6. *With particular reference to Act 3 Scene 3, examine the techniques that Iago uses to persuade Othello of Desdemona's guilt.*

7. *Act 3 Scene 3 marks the turning point in Othello. The scene begins with Othello expressing his love for Desdemona, but, influenced by Iago's poisonous insinuations, he ends by wanting to kill her. Through a close examination of this scene, discuss how this change comes about.*

8. *Is Othello a tragic victim or is he in any way responsible for his own fate?*

9 Write a review of a film version of Othello *that you have seen.*
Choose two or three key scenes and explore their presentation,
comparing them with your own views on how you think they
should be interpreted and performed.

10 *Examine the effects created by Shakespeare's use of imagery in*
Othello.

11 *Some critics have called this play a 'domestic tragedy' because it*
does not deal with the big, fundamental issues but focuses on
the relationship between a man and his wife. Do you think that
this is a fair description of the play, or does the play deal with
broader issues?

12 *Do you think Desdemona is presented as an innocent and*
passive victim, or is there more to Shakespeare's presentation of
her than this?

13 *Examine the ways in which Othello's language changes*
throughout the play to reflect the changes in his emotional state.

14 *Discuss the ways in which the differences between appearance*
and reality are important in Othello.

15   *How do you respond to the presentation of Cassio in* Othello?

16 *How true do you find Othello's description of himself as 'one not*
easily jealous, but being wrought,/Perplexed in the extreme.'

17 *How is the idea that Othello is an 'outsider' figure important to*
the play?

In order to write an effective essay, you need to approach your task in an organised way. You need to **plan** your essay carefully before beginning to write. This will help you to achieve a higher grade.

- The first thing to do is read the question carefully to make sure that you fully understand it, then highlight key words.

- You will need to make notes on the topic in order to start preparing your ideas. You can do this in various ways, such as making a list of key points, or creating a spidergram or a mind map.

- One advantage of using mind maps or spidergrams is that they help you to create links between the various points you make. Put the title of the essay in the middle of a page and add your points around it. You can then draw lines to connect up various points or ideas, linking them in a clear, visual way.

- If you wish, you can colour code your ideas, or even add pictures or symbols if that helps you to think about your ideas more clearly.

- Since mind maps and spidergrams are a way of charting your knowledge, they are also an excellent revision aid. You could work through a number of essay titles in this way. (See some examples of spidergrams on the following pages.)

- In the planning stage of your essay, it is also a good idea to jot down some useful quotations. These should be kept brief and to the point, and can be added to your spidergram.

- It can also be useful to plan what you are going to write in each paragraph of your essay. You can number the branches on your spidergram, so that you are clear about the order of your points. This will help you to structure your work more effectively.

- Remember that you are much more likely to write an effective essay if you do some planning before you start to write it.

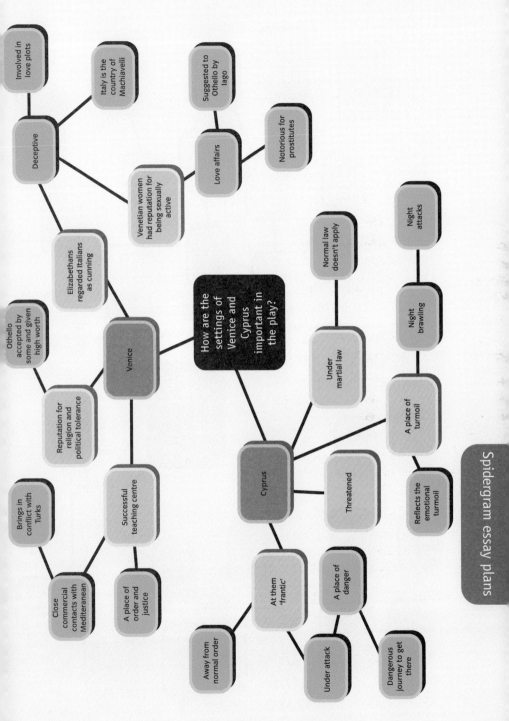

How are the settings of Venice and Cyprus important in the play?

Venice
- Deceptive
  - Involved in love plots
  - Italy is the country of Machiavelli
- Venetian women had reputation for being sexually active
  - Love affairs
    - Suggested to Othello by Iago
    - Notorious for prostitutes
- Elizabethans regarded Italians as cunning
- Reputation for religion and political tolerance
  - Othello accepted by some and given high worth
- Successful teaching centre
  - Brings in conflict with Turks
  - Close commercial contacts with Mediteranean
  - A place of order and justice

Cyprus
- Under martial law
  - Normal law doesn't apply
- A place of turmoil
  - Night brawling
    - Night attacks
  - Reflects the emotional turmoil
- Threatened
- At them 'frantic'
  - Away from normal order
  - Under attack
- A place of danger
  - Dangerous journey to get there

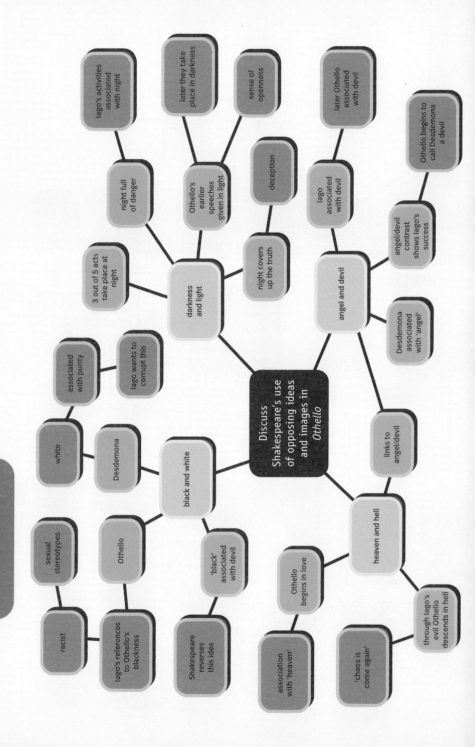

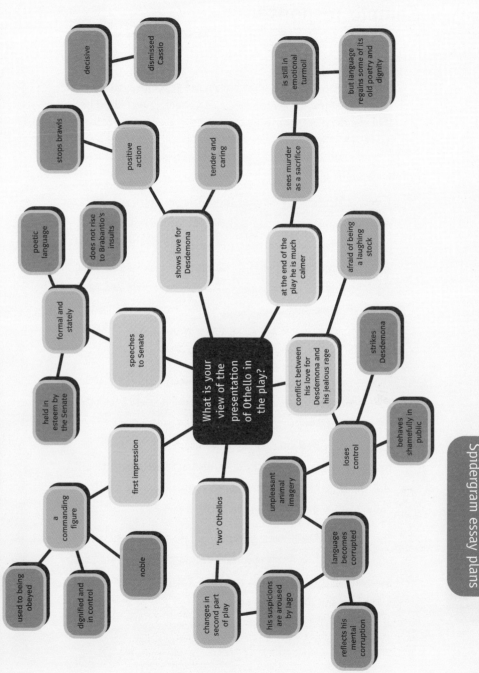

What is your view of the presentation of Othello in the play?

- decisive
  - dismissed Cassio
- positive action
  - stops brawls
  - decisive
  - tender and caring
- shows love for Desdemona
  - positive action
  - tender and caring
- is still in emotional turmoil
  - but language regains some of its old poetry and dignity
- sees murder as a sacrifice
- at the end of the play he is much calmer
- afraid of being a laughing stock
- speeches to Senate
  - formal and stately
    - poetic language
    - does not rise to Brabantio's insults
    - held in esteem by the Senate
- conflict between his love for Desdemona and his jealous rage
  - strikes Desdemona
  - loses control
    - behaves shamefully in public
- first impression
  - a commanding figure
    - used to being obeyed
    - dignified and in control
    - noble
- 'two' Othellos
  - changes in second part of play
  - his suspicions are aroused by Iago
  - unpleasant animal imagery
  - language becomes corrupted
    - reflects his mental corruption

Spidergram essay plans

73

Sample response

Read carefully Othello's speech from Act 1, Scene 3, starting 'Her father loved me, oft invited me...' and ending 'And I loved her, that she did pity them.' How does Othello use language to express his ideas both here and elsewhere in the play? You should refer to this speech and one or two examples from other parts of the play.

The main character in the play, Othello, is presented in many ways. When we first hear Iago and Roderigo speak of Othello the reader is told that he isn't a very nice character, and they speak of him with little respect. ✔ This is shown when Iago speaks of Othello as 'his Moorship'. ✔ Moor is used as an offensive term and paired with 'ship' is mocking the authority he has. Not only is Othello presented as a person that lacks authority but also one who is unpopular and disliked.

This is contradicted later on in the play when Othello is explaining how he and Desdemona fell in love. ✔ In this part of the play Othello is seen to be much more respected as he speaks of how he was invited by Brabantio to his house to tell him stories. If Brabantio didn't respect Othello he wouldn't have invited him. It also shows that he must have gained respect from the people around him if they are willing to listen to him. ✔

The language Othello uses presents him as well educated. ✔ He uses words such as 'Anthropophagi' instead of a simple word such as 'cannibal'. The tone of this speech is also gentle. Othello is not worked up and the way it is written suggests it is to be read slowly, and this shows that Othello is calm. ✔

This speech also shows Othello as an honest, truthful character as he backs up what he is saying by making it descriptive: 'greedy ear'. ✓ Othello is also seen as being a modest character as he describes himself as 'rude' in his speech. This speech also presents Othello as a gentleman, ✓ as he speaks highly of Desdemona and Brabantio throughout, and he also says he's shocked that Desdemona liked him and she liked him for who he was.

Later on in the play a different Othello is presented to the audience, one who is corrupted by lies and one appearing violent. This Othello also speaks differently from the character we met before. ✓ His speeches are not as long and poetic, his tone is more harsh and he isn't as descriptive or using as much imagery.

Throughout the play Othello is presented as the 'good guy', but he is corrupted by Iago who is manipulative. ✓

Examiner's comments

This is a sound response which deals well with the question and makes some relevant points. The opening part of the response could be more sharply focused on the actual question, though. The student then goes on to make some relevant points about the language used in the passage and supports her ideas with appropriate textual references. To improve the grade further this part of the question should be more detailed and focus on specific examples of language use. Colloquialisms such 'good guy' should also be avoided.

Sample response

Read carefully Othello's speech from Act 1, Scene 3, starting 'Her father loved me, oft invited me...' and ending 'And I loved her, that she did pity them.' How does Othello use language to express his ideas both here and elsewhere in the play? You should refer to this speech and one or two examples from other parts of the play.

Throughout the play Othello, the audience is shown different sides of characters and how they act towards each other. Othello himself is a character who Shakespeare develops as our impressions of him change throughout the play. ✔

The poetic language used by Othello in this extract is very positive, ✔ whereas his views of later situations are still shown to the audience through very poetic language, but they contrast greatly with the current situation and create negative images. Othello uses words like 'wondrous', 'heaven', 'loved' and 'youth' to describe how his relationship with Desdemona began. ✔ These words are used by Shakespeare to make Othello seem very caring and fond of Desdemona.

However, this is not the case when Iago's devious and scheming tricks eventually convince Othello that Desdemona is having an affair. Othello becomes blinded by rage and because of this his language changes. ✔ Instead of loving, caring words he describes Desdemona as a 'impudent strumpet' and 'cunning whore of Venice', ✔ which both refer to Desdemona as being a whore who can't be faithful to anyone, which is why Othello decides to kill her.

Another key theme that can be found in the extract that shows Othello's character is that of military speech. ✔ I think that Shakespeare chooses to use this to make Othello sound like a leader, and to show that he has lots of experience. Many references are made to his time as a soldier, such as 'battles, sieges', 'the imminent deadly breach', and 'being taken by the insolent foe'. ✓ Elsewhere in the play, both before and after this extract, Othello again uses military speech and actions to control the situation. A good example of this is when he breaks up the fight involving Cassio. Here he uses words like 'hold for your lives!', which again shows his power with his voice which he uses in the extract to persuade the Duke. ✓

To conclude on the way that Othello is presented throughout the play is difficult because the views of him change during the play as the plot develops. His power and presence are continuous though, even though his power is put to bad use when he kills Desdemona. Another clever technique used by Shakespeare is that other characters influence the actions of Othello and the way he is presented to the audience, especially Iago. ✓

Examiner's comments

The student begins with a brief indication of the ways in which Othello's character is presented through the language he uses and then moves on to make some specific points about the passage. The student then returns to the given passage and makes some further analytical points about the language used here, comparing these with how Othello uses language in another part of the play. A little more analysis of the other parts of the play selected would have improved the answer further. Also, the conclusion could have been a little more focused.

Quick quiz answers

Quick quiz 1
Uncover the plot
1   Roderigo; Iago
2   hates his master; Brabantio.
3   Iago; witchcraft
4   Cyprus
5   after; Iago
6   Roderigo; Cassio; lover

Who? What? Why? When? Where? How?
1   Brabantio's description of his daughter seems in error because she appears soon after this to defend her husband boldly and declare her love for him.
2   'men whose heads / Do grow beneath their shoulders' (presumably great apes)
3   107; 140; 200 (then join with 30 more)
4   Brabantio
5   Iago says this to Roderigo.

Who said that?
1   Roderigo (1,1)
2   Othello (1,2)
3   Desdemona, answering her father's question as to whom she owes most obedience (1,3)
4   Iago, talking to Roderigo (1,3)
5   Iago, talking to Brabantio (1,1)

Quick quiz 2
Uncover the plot
1   Iago; Cassio
2   Roderigo
3   consummation; Cassio
4   Cassio; Roderigo
5   Iago; Cassio; Montano
6   Iago

Who? What? Why? When? Where? How?
1   Iago
2   Roderigo
3   Cassio
4   Montano
5   Roderigo complains to Iago about this.
6   Desdemona, according to Iago

Who said that?
1   Iago (2,1)
2   Iago, talking about Cassio (2,1)
3   Iago (2,3)
4   Desdemona (2,1)
5   Iago (2,1)
6   Othello (2,3)

Quick quiz 3
Uncover the plot
1   Cassio
2   plead for; Othello
3   jealousy
4   Iago
5   in his sleep; beard

Who? What? Why? When? Where? How?
1   the handkerchief that Othello gave to Desdemona
2   Cassio
3   Iago says he will put it there for Cassio to find.
4   Cassio and Bianca
5   an Egyptian charmer
6   he had a toothache

Who said that?
1   Iago (3,3)
2   Emilia (3,3)
3   Emilia (3,3)

4 Cassio (3,4)

5 Iago (3,3)

6 Othello, to Desdemona, who has just left (3,3)

Quick quiz 4
Uncover the plot

1 admitted; faints

2 spy on; Bianca

3 Lodovico; Venice; Cassio.

4 strikes; unkind

5 Emilia; ignores

Who? What? Why? When? Where? How?

1 Roderigo

2 weeping

3 to dismiss Emilia from her room

4 Mauritania

5 Lodovico's and Iago's

Who said that?

1 Iago, to Othello (4,1)

2 Othello (4,1)

3 Othello (4,2)

4 Iago (4,2)

5 Othello (4,2)

Quick quiz 5
Uncover the plot

1 Bianca; Cassio; Roderigo

2 Cassio; Iago

3 destroy her beauty

4 handkerchief; smothers

5 stabs; dies

6 Cassio; refuses to speak

Who? What? Why? When? Where? How?

1 that he allow her 'But a half an hour, but while I say one prayer!'

2 Iago and Roderigo

3 'Commend me to my kind lord, O, farewell!'

4 grief

5 Emilia

6 Iago

Who said that?

1 Iago, of Bianca (5,1)

2 Emilia (5,2)

3 Gratiano (5,2)

4 Emilia (5,2)

5 Emilia (5,2)

6 Roderigo (5,1)

Page 18, Shakespeare, © Robert Harding World Imagery/
Robert Harding Picture Library/Alamy.Com
Page 21, Scene, © Kelly-Mooney Photography/Corbis

First published 1995
Revised edition 2004

Letts Educational
Chiswick Centre
414 Chiswick High Road
London W4 5TF
Tel: 020 8996 3333

Text © Stewart Martin 1995
2004 edition revised by Steven Croft

Cover and text design by Hardlines Ltd., Charlbury, Oxfordshire.

Typeset by Letterpart Ltd., Reigate, Surrey.

Graphic illustration by Beehive Illustration, Cirencester, Gloucestershire.

Commissioned by Cassandra Birmingham

Editorial project management by Jo Kemp

Printed in Italy.

Design and illustration © Letts Educational Ltd

British Library Cataloguing in Publication Data. A CIP record of this book is
available from the British Library.

ISBN 1 84315 322 X

Letts Educational is a division of Granada Learning, part of Granada plc.